Living Sacrifices
A Missionary Odyssey

LIVING SACRIFICES

A MISSIONARY ODYSSEY

JESSE C. FLETCHER

BROADMAN PRESS ■ Nashville, Tennessee

© 1974 • Broadman Press
Nashville, Tennessee
4272-10
ISBN: 0-8054-7210-x

Dewey Decimal Classification: B
Library of Congress Catalog Card number: 73-93903
Printed in the United States of America

To
John D. Barbee
who first interpreted
for me
the mystery of call
and the possibility of ministry

Acknowledgements

Biography inevitably leaves the author with mixed feelings about his own contribution. Obviously, it is the life of his subject that is the essence of the story. No biographer, however skilled, can make a nonnotable life notable. Ultimately, any honor must go to the one who lived out the story.

Further confounding any pretentions on the part of a biographer is the inevitability of collaborators, i.e., informants, researchers, reporters, and editors. This biography, the story of two lives, includes many collaborators.

This author, therefore, acknowledges a debt to many people. First of all, there is a debt to the Abernathys. They lived out with courage and commitment the exciting missionary odyssey that follows. Also, two people had already plowed this ground and the marks of their furrows made the task much easier: Rosalee Mills Appleby's unpublished manuscript on John Abernathy and Dollie Hiett's unpublished manuscript on Jewell Abernathy were indispensable guides in the research task.

In this project the author has compounded a growing debt to research assistant Marilyn Glazebrook, who was not only that but also editor and typist. She worked with the author on each of his five previous books and he probably would not attempt such a project without her.

Another veteran co-worker in previous efforts also contributed to this biography. Genevieve Greer, recently retired book editor of the Foreign Mission Board, graciously read the manuscript and made many helpful suggestions.

Timothy Cho's excellent doctoral dissertation on the Korean Baptist Convention, Charles Culpepper's personal reminiscence and his book on the Shantung revival, and an interpretation of Korean events by Don Jones, missionary in Korea and colleague of the Abernathys, were indispensable. The research help of Mrs. Grace Kainakian and Miss Nell Stanley of the Foreign Mission Board and the comments of Mrs. Baker J. Cauthen, who was born in China, were most helpful.

The author would also like to express profound appreciation for the information and interpretation supplied by colleagues Winston Crawley and Baker J. Cauthen. Both men lived through many of the events recorded and their help was invaluable.

The author's goal was to let the Abernathys' lives speak for themselves through the faithful recreation of their time frame and the events they experienced. In doing so he has tried to avoid either editorializing or eulogizing.

JESSE C. FLETCHER

Richmond, Virginia
March 18, 1974

Contents

I beseech you therefore, brethren, by the mercies of God, that ye present your bodies a living sacrifice, holy, acceptable unto God, which is your reasonable service.

—Romans 12:1

1
China Mail

John Arch Abernathy motioned with his hand to catch the eye of the newsboy walking through the crowded train. The boy brought a paper. John stood up, reached a thumb and forefinger into his vest pocket, extracted five pennies, and paid for it. The Kansas City *Star* was a lot more newspaper than he was used to. It was larger even than the Charlotte Sunday paper his dad received through the mail back home in North Carolina. Bigger even than the Fort Worth *Star Telegram* John read during his years at Southwestern Baptist Seminary in Texas.

He sat down again in the hard leather coach seat and adjusted his five-foot-eight-inch frame with its compact 170 pounds into a more comfortable position before thumbing through the paper.

That August day in 1920 the newspaper was not shy on news. The Bolshevik Revolution continued in Russia. The 19th amendment was nearly a reality, and along with it, new status for women. John wasn't sure how he felt about woman's suffrage. Probably okay.

The literary section revealed that English author, H. G. Wells, had written an *Outline of History* and Sinclair Lewis had published a new book called *Main Street*.

He glanced at the account of the wedding of Mary Pickford and Douglas Fairbanks. John wasn't much on movies. He read carefully the wrap-up stories from the 1920 Olympics held at Antwerp.

Self-consciously, John rubbed the back of his hand across the stub of a beard that was beginning to accumulate. He had boarded the train to Hiddenite, North Carolina, for a journey that had carried him a day and a night through the green fullness of an Appalachian summer, across the hills and streams of Tennessee, through eastern Kentucky and Missouri to Kansas City. The train was not to be in

Kansas City long. It would take on coal and water, and as soon as the passengers boarded, it would be on its way with half of the United States still to be crossed: the Rockies, the Nevada and California deserts, the Sierras, and into the great city of San Francisco.

On his way to China as a Baptist missionary, John Arch Abernathy found what he was looking for on a back page of the newspaper Civil war continued in China. There were growing tensions over the granting of concessions in Shantung Province to the Japanese. Sun Yat-sen's efforts to unite the country were making little headway. Reports of threats to missionaries raised specters of the bloody reprisals during the Boxer Rebellion twenty years before.

John pressed down the hint of anxiety that crept into his stomach. He had heard that more than two hundred missionaries and twenty thousand Chinese converts were murdered during that terrible rebellion. He had been reading about China for a long time. Eleven years before, in 1909, after a returned China missionary talked to John's church in North Carolina, God laid China on his heart in a way that said, "I want you there."

He had felt anxiety then, too, but time dulled the feeling. John had seen himself as a missionary for several years. Now, in a little over a month he would be sailing into Shanghai and actually doing what he had dreamed about for so long.

He folded the newspaper in time to catch sight of a middle-aged man trying to squeeze several valises and boxes above the seat across from him. Behind the man a young woman stood helplessly, the narrow aisle blocking any help she might offer. John Arch judged her to be in her twenties and the man to be her father.

Affably, John said, "Let me help you."

In a few minutes everything was stored and John Arch introduced himself.

"Glad to know you, and thank you for the help," Frank Leonard said. "This is my daughter Zenobia. We're from Arkansas."

"I'm from North Carolina," John smiled. "I know some good people from Arkansas."

John's eye caught sight of the Hotel Stewart, San Francisco, tag on the luggage. He exclaimed, "Why, that's where I'm going!" Then he noticed the transfer tag to the USS *China Mail.* "And that's my ship! You're going to China!"

The young woman grinned and said, "You must be a missionary, too."

John liked her smile and the big eyes that danced behind round steel-rimmed glasses.

Their meeting with the stranger took the edge off an obviously difficult time for the father and daughter. She was his eldest child, one on whom he had depended heavily since the death of his wife six years earlier, and he was struggling with the leave-taking. Frank Leonard was relieved that the young man would be accompanying his daughter, but the thought of seven years before he would see her again was almost too much to bear. Their only time apart had been the previous year when she was in school in Ada, Oklahoma. That had seemed a lifetime.

But Frank Leonard knew God had called his daughter to China; he knew she was sure. He had laid the whole matter before the Lord many times in prayer, kneeling beside his bed and behind the horse and plow in the furrows on his Arkansas farm. He had tried to steel himself for the separation that now was here.

Sensing the difficulty the father was having, John turned back to his seat discreetly after muttering best wishes and offering to be of any help he could. He picked up the newspaper again and put it down only to wave as Mr. Leonard left the train.

The train lurched and squealed and they were on their way. John gave the young lady a reassuring grin and she smiled back. Her eyes were full; John hurt for her.

He did not have the same problem, though he wished he did. His own father had died in 1914 in an influenza epidemic. Though John was eighteen at the time and attending the University of North Carolina, the loss had been a heavy blow to him. His commitment to China and the demands of the rural church he served as pastor kept him going.

By the time their train pulled into San Francisco two days later, the two young missionaries-to-be had discovered a lot about each other. It was good to have a friend on the journey ahead.

The USS *China Mail,* most of her crew, and many of her passengers had crossed the Pacific many times. That alleviated their anxiety, but it also dissipated their excitement. Anyone watching the animated faces of John Arch Abernathy and Zenobia Jewell Leonard as their "slow boat to China" pulled out of San Francisco harbor would have certainly opted for the excitement of a first crossing. Emotions of leaving their homeland had been dealt with when they boarded the train, one in North Carolina and the other in Arkansas. The gears of their life were in forward now and their blossoming friendship was an added tonic to their inherently bouyant natures.

Almost as soon as they sailed, the gentle roll of the ship and the swell of the blue Pacific—ordinarily symbols of romance and tranquility—precipitated a queasiness in Zenobia. It quickly accelerated into the most miserable kind of seasickness. She retired to her bed to toss about in a state of semi-reality.

In her more lucid moments Zenobia's mind raced back to the summer revival in her home church when she had argued with the Lord about being a missionary. Wryly, she remembered telling God she was not a good traveler; she even became sick on trains. She had told the Lord she would not be able to survive the boat trip. Now she was sure of it.

She repeated Philippians 4:19 over and over again. "But my God shall supply all your need according to his riches in glory by Christ Jesus." Then the sickness would engulf her feeble efforts to reach out in faith. Between spasms of nausea her mind held tightly to the words of 2 Corinthians 12:9, "My grace is sufficient for thee."

In the lonely travail of her stateroom, she repeated Matthew 28:20, "Lo, I am with you alway, even unto the end of the world," reminding herself that since the Lord had promised to walk with her in everything, he was with her in this.

After a day, one of the missionary women secured medicine for her that brought some relief. Others came to express concern. The captain of the ship visited her sympathetically.

Then John came and led her from her cabin to the comfort of a deck chair. "You'll get better quick here in the sunshine," he said.

The trip was to take twenty-nine days with stops in Hawaii and Japan. The weather was good, and once Zenobia recovered, the perfect sunsets that marked the end of each day were avidly enjoyed by the young travelers.

"When did God call you to China, Zenobia?" the warm smile and squared, handsome features of her young inquisitor were an incentive, but it took little urging for Zenobia to share her "testimony."

"A little over a year ago I knew for sure," she replied, "but I believe God began the process when I was fourteen years of age and trusted the Lord Jesus as my Savior."

She turned from John's understanding attention to the luminescent waves, swelling and falling in the moonlight as if to recreate the scene she was recalling.

"Where I went to church, we had preaching every fourth Sunday and a revival every summer. During the revival that summer I was burdened because I knew I needed Jesus Christ, but I didn't know what to do. I confessed my sins. I prayed asking for his forgiveness. I asked him to come into my heart. But nothing happened. Finally, at the end of the third night I told him that I had done everything I knew how to do and it was up to him. At that minute I had the most wonderful assurance of my salvation and it flowed through all my being."

John smiled in a way that told her he knew exactly what she was talking about.

"I told my father," she said, "and the next night at preaching, I made a public profession of faith."

John said, "I'll bet you were baptized in a creek."

She smiled, "How did you know?"

"I'm a country boy," John laughed knowingly.

Zenobia said, "I was baptized in a creek, and from that point on I have tried to live for my Lord. Since we got to go to church only every fourth Sunday, I didn't grow as a Christian as I should have. We didn't have Sunday School or any missionary organizations."

John prompted, "But you didn't know you were going to be a missionary until last year, you said."

"That's right. In the summer revival I began to ask myself if I would be willing to go to the foreign field if God should call me. I must confess that I trembled at the thought.

"In September I went to East Central State College in Ada, Oklahoma. The church there had a 'call out the called' emphasis in October, and I knew that God wanted me to go to China. Things developed so quickly that my head is still spinning.

"I was introduced to Mr. Blalock of the China Direct Mission. I agreed to go to China if he would help me find support. So, here I am," she grinned and then giggled a bit, a little unsure of herself after talking so long. She wanted her newfound friend to understand.

"How did God call you?" she asked him.

"My trip started like yours, but a lot earlier. We had laid by our crops in the summer of 1909 when our church—the South River Church—had its 'protracted' meeting. The evangelist preached on the text, 'All have sinned and come short of the glory of God.' My cousin seated next to me asked if I wanted to be a Christian. The next thing I knew tears were running down my cheeks and I was kneeling at 'the mourners' bench,' as we called it. My father came and knelt by me. He urged me to trust Christ and I did. I have never had reason to doubt that experience."

John stopped a moment, savoring the memory.

"A year later in the same church a China missionary, Dr. W. C. Tyree, talked about the millions in China who had never heard of Jesus Christ. Even though I was only thirteen, I felt that God wanted me to preach—and wanted me to preach in China."

John looked at Zenobia to see if she understood. Her eyes were bright with wetness.

The two young missionaries were not always together. Not sure of their own feelings or of how their friendship appeared to others, they avoided that.

After reading the Bible and praying, a habit she had followed strictly for a number of years, Zenobia often went to a quiet section of the deck to sort out her feelings. Despite the companionship of the athletic young North Carolinian and others in the ship's company, she missed her father sorely.

She remembered the day he gave her a horse and buggy to make the five-mile round trip to high school. He also encouraged her when she took the county test for a teacher's certificate, and told her how proud he was when she began teaching.

She thought about the day in 1916 when word came that her mother had died. It had been only three months after the birth of the sixth child in the family. Zenobia quit teaching to become sister-mother to five younger brothers and sisters, including the three-month old boy.

Zenobia threw herself into the task with great energy and with good humor. The father-daughter relationship grew even closer. But it was a healthy closeness, and the daughter rejoiced when in 1919 the father wooed and won a new mate. That freed Zenobia to begin her long postponed college education in Ada, Oklahoma, where she experienced the call to foreign missions. It did not seem possible that in less than one year from that date she was crossing the waters of the Pacific toward the storied Middle Kingdom.

Friends insisted that she was foolish to go to China without a husband. "If God wants me to have a husband, he'll bring one along in due time," she responded firmly.

Twenty-six now, she wondered if God wanted her to have a husband. If he did, would it be someone like John Arch Abernathy? Catching sight of John's gregarious form moving among the other passengers, she would chastise herself for such presumptuous thoughts.

Of course, John Abernathy was not without his own moments of reflection and mixed emotions. He hoped he was not rushing the Lord in going to China at this time. Rather than stay on at Southwestern Seminary to finish his theological education along with his friend, Charles Culpepper, and others who were pointed for China and who planned to seek appointment with the Southern Baptist Convention's Foreign Mission Board, John had taken appointment with the China Direct Mission. He knew that controversy had brought that group into being as a split from Southern Baptists, and he did not want to divorce himself from his Southern Baptist brethren by such an appointment. But his sense of urgency was strong. If souls were dying without hope in China, how could he justify waiting?

It had been so long since he told God he would preach in China that waiting any longer seemed intolerable. The wait had been hard enough during the war years while he was getting his education.

Since he was obviously a healthy young man, he had often had to explain to people why he wasn't in France. As a young minister he did not have the education to be a chaplain; yet, he could not lay aside his calling to pick up a gun. During the summers he worked in a steel mill in Detroit, followed the wheat harvest in Nebraska, and worked as a common laborer at Camp Benning, Georgia. Through it all, he renewed his sense of direction with thoughts of China and an appetite for information of any kind about the land to which God was calling him.

"You will need a mate, John," his sister advised him.

"God will give me a mate in due time," he replied.

Women friends had always been abundant, though John's social skills were modest. He enjoyed the company of young Christian women. But a mate? No one like that had come along yet. Maybe she would be someone like his new young Arkansas friend with the big grin and laughing eyes. He liked her blend of dedication and good humor. And he liked being with her. But he reminded himself that the appearance of things was important. He would need to limit their times together.

John and Zenobia were part of a group of six missionaries going out as appointees of the China Direct Mission. Their leader, Dr. T. L. Blalock, had recruited each of them. Often he gathered the group for orientation about the country to which they were going and about the turbulent times that seemed to engulf it all too frequently.

Sometimes during the voyage they met with other missionaries, some new but many returning to China. One of the veteran missionaries led in Bible studies for the new missionaries. Both John Abernathy and Zenobia Leonard loved the Scriptures and listened with rapt attention. Afterwards they would talk about China.

From the older missionaries, John and his colleagues learned they were going to a land with history rich beyond anything their meager studies had yet revealed to them.

"Don't let the peasantry of China and their illiteracy deceive you," one older missionary said. "China may have the longest continuous history of any nation. While the civilization of Abraham predates anything uncovered in China, those civilizations have perished. China continues."

The new missionaries listened attentively as their mentor told them of China's history. They learned that during the time Moses was leading the children of Israel from Egypt, the Shang Dynasty flourished in China's Yellow River Valley. The older man reminded them that the Chou Dynasty was extending its power to the Yangtze Valley and giving birth to such wise men as Confucius during the time David and Solomon were in their glory in biblical history.

"The Chous maintained their hold through the days of Alexander the Great," he said, "before giving way to the ambitious Han Dynasty during the time of Christ. The Hans built their own empire throughout Asia in counterpart to the Roman Empire," he pointed out.

"The emperors of the Sui Dynasty were building a transportation

network in Asia when Europe was floundering in the Dark Ages,"
he said. "There was a culture flowering under the T'ang Dynasty
hundreds of years before the European Renaissance."

"What of the Mongols?" John asked.

"They flourished during the great Yüan Dynasty," the missionary
answered. "You probably remember their most famous emperor,
Kublai Khan.

"It was in Kublai Khan's day that China began to encounter the
rest of the world," the missionary continued, "and the Ming Dynasty,
which ruled after the Yüans, began sending great fleets abroad to
trade with other nations."

"Was this the dynasty Sun Yat-sen overthrew?" one asked.

"No, Dr. Sun overthrew the Manchus," the narrator replied. "They
took over about the year 1644 as invaders from the North and really
constituted an alien rule."

The older missionary paused, then said, "But it wasn't Sun Yat-sen
who overthrew the Manchu Dynasty so much as it was the foreign
interests in China."

One of the new missionaries asked, "Was that the Boxer Rebellion?"

Again the teacher paused as if remembering the terror raised by
the very term.

"Yes and no," he replied. "You really have to go back to 1842
and what is called the 'Opium War' and the 'Treaty of Nanking.'
Defeated by Western powers, China was forced to open five ports
for trading and to cede Hong Kong to Great Britain. In addition,
the Western powers received legal jurisdiction over their own nationals
in China. In 1858 they forced still further concessions from China.

"Of course, this opened doors to China and made possible the
development of many great leaders such as Sun Yat-sen. So, while
it was heavy on China, it has in some ways worked out to be a blessing.

"But the Manchus continued to resent the foreign encroachment.
Agitation against any foreign or Christian element began in 1898
and culminated in 1900 with the horror of the Boxer Rebellion when
the foreign legations were invaded, and missionaries and Chinese
Christians were murdered all over the land. The foreign nations put
down the rebellion and made the Chinese pay an immense indemnity."

The missionary paused. Zenobia felt that his sentiments were mixed.

"The result was further domination by China by Western nations.

But it did help Sun Yat-sen and others overcome the Manchu Dynasty in 1911, though they have not been able to unify China. Dr. Sun is still trying through his Kuomintang Party."

One of the travelers took sharp issue with the implication that the Western encroachments had been good for China. "If China's culture is so old and so commendable, why would we assume that our new culture with its industrial horrors is a plus for China?"

A young lady spoke up firmly, "Don't forget that it has enabled the gospel to enter China. And without the gospel, China has nothing."

"But with the gospel has come gunboats, disease, the breaking down of the central government, and the appearance of warlords," the traveler said.

"Nonsense," she replied, "there have been warlords in China since time immemorial."

John and Zenobia talked at length that night about what they had heard.

"Dr. Blalock says there are battles going on right now in the area where we are to live," Zenobia said.

John replied, "Yes, but I believe the Kuomintang will be able to unify China . . . ," he stopped, and then continued, "if the Japanese do not press their military ambitions any further."

Realizing he was touching new ground, John paused. "One of the missionaries going to Japan tells me that the Japanese militarists are gaining control in Japan and that one day they will attempt to bring all of China under their dominion," he explained.

"Do you believe that?" Zenobia asked, wide-eyed.

"I don't know," he replied. "Others have tried to conquer China and have been swallowed up in the process. But Japan is an aggressive and industrially progressive nation."

John looked at her and smiled. "God has not called us to worry about governments and treaties and uprisings and wars; he called us to preach the gospel to these people that they might have the light of Jesus Christ. Christ can make a difference that no warlord or leader can frustrate."

"You are right, John!" she exclaimed. "Listening to all that we heard today has left my head swimming. But I know why I am on this boat at this moment. God is leading me to China, and he can handle the details."

As the USS *China Mail* continued westward, John Abernathy had his first opportunity to witness to an Asian. A well-educated Hindu man from India was returning from his studies in the United States. John got to know the man, and as the days passed, tried to convince him of Christian truth. The Hindu man in turn made a very learned defense of his own religious beliefs, finding in John a willing listener. John wanted to understand his Asian friend's thoughts and needs, but his heart ached for him to know Christ. John's entreaties brought no visible results, however.

Later, as John told Zenobia of his efforts, he said, "People are not going to respond automatically to the message just because we cross an ocean to bring it."

Privately, John resolved to become as articulate an ambassador for his Lord as possible. The encounter with the Hindu man made him realize he had a long way to go.

For both John and Zenobia the sea voyage was a combination of rest and restlessness: rest in that the limits of the ship imposed time that could be brought up in reflection and repose, and restlessness in that there was a building anticipation for China and the life to which they had been called.

Brief stopovers in Hawaii and Japan offered respite from both rest and restlessness. Japan especially engaged their attention, not only because its aggressiveness and rapid industrialization were becoming the wonder of Asia, but because in Japan they faced for the first time the population trauma of Asia. Hordes of people seemed to line every bit of space.

The final leg of the voyage led from Japan across the China Sea and up China's Hwang Poo River to Shanghai. They landed there one bright steamy morning.

After making sure the young women in the group were cared for, John left the ship. He was one of the first passengers to set foot in China.

"The moment I touched Chinese soil," he wrote later, "God seemed to say to me, though there was no audible voice, 'Now you are where I want you.' Peace came into my heart. If there had ever been a doubt about my call as a missionary, there was none now."

Zenobia's sentiment and emotions allowed her no time for such feelings. She was overwhelmed with the plight of the coolies carrying giant trunks from the ship.

"Why must so many people be little more than beasts of burden?" she thought. Her heart reached out to the people, and the love for them that began then dominated the days and years before her.

The new missionaries spent their first night on Chinese soil in Shanghai. An older missionary invited them, along with some of the returning missionaries, to be his guests at a well-known restaurant for their first Chinese meal. The table was steaming—an experience for the nostrils as well as for the eyes. Bird's nest soup, shark fin, garlic, spices, and sauces of every variety were overwhelming. In spite of their amazement, and some dismay, the new missionaries were able to laugh. One of the young women tried to eat the food and then, gagging, left the table. Zenobia knew the woman was in distress, and followed. When she found her, the young woman was weeping and near hysteria.

"How can I ever live here when the food is like this?" the woman cried. "I shall die." Zenobia, trying to comfort her, was grateful she had not had a similar reaction. Her taste buds had responded in the same manner as had her heart.

As Zenobia returned to the dining room, she reassured the group. "She's all right. She'll be back in just a moment."

Then she caught John Abernathy's eyes. A bond of understanding passed between them. She knew John appreciated her efforts to help the young woman. His look made her glad she had tried.

2
Confucius' Mountain

Though John Abernathy and Zenobia Leonard were both Southern Baptists, the mission group sponsoring them was the product of a bitter split with the Southern Baptist Foreign Mission Board. The controversy had begun in North China where Southern Baptist missionaries opened work after the War Between the States. J. Landrum Holmes and his wife opened the work in the newly opened treaty port of Chefoo during the bloody T'ai P'ing rebellion against the ruling Manchu Dynasty.

Two years after the Holmeses took up their work in Chefoo, rebels laid seige to the city. Landrum Holmes and an Anglican missionary courageously volunteered to go to the rebel camp to plead for the city's safety. Their brutalized bodies were found eight days later.

The development of the work in North China was renewed two years later when missionary T. P. Crawford began work in Tengchow.

In the late 1880's Crawford began to feud with the Foreign Mission Board's administration over mission methods. He held that the Board should not give financial help to native Chinese workers, or construct buildings, or open schools to be supported with mission funds. He called instead for missionaries to give themselves solely to itinerate preaching.

While the Board was sympathetic with Crawford's points of view, it felt it should give its missionaries latitude to adopt whatever strategies seemed needed. The board would not draw the strict guidelines Crawford advocated.

As a result, Crawford and others who sympathized with him withdrew from the Southern Baptist Convention's Foreign Mission Board. They advocated the support of missionaries by individual churches or groups of churches and urged the missionaries to adopt Chinese dress and follow his methods. Thus began what was called the Gospel Mission Movement. One result was the Chinese Direct Mission under which John Abernathy and Zenobia Leonard went to China in 1920.

John Abernathy knew something of the controversy, but felt that the differences had receded and that there was a healthy fellowship between those who went under the sponsorship of the China Direct Mission and those who went under the Foreign Mission Board.

The China Direct Mission sent both John and Zenobia to Taian to begin language study. Most of the China Direct missionaries were quartered in a compound with senior missionaries of their mission, but there was not enough room for all. John and Zenobia were housed in the same compound with the Frank Connelys, who were Southern Baptist missionaries.

Language school was the living room of one of the senior missionaries at the China Direct Mission compound. On the first day of school the nine students were greeted by three teachers—old Chinese gentlemen dressed in long flowing robes, their hands crossed before them and tucked in the full sleeves. The teachers greeted their students by moving their hands in a way that caused Zenobia to say, "I was sure they were shaking hands with themselves." Then the teachers with just a suggestion of a smile, bowed slowly. Thus the students were to know that they were welcome and that the teachers were delighted to be with them.

There were no books. The teachers pointed to an object such as an eye or the nose or the mouth and slowly pronounced the Chinese word for it. The students then repeated the word. They soon discovered that tone was everything and that there were four tones.

The first day presented a delicate problem for the teachers. How should they address the unmarried missionary women? They could not address them by the word for an unmarried Chinese because that implied an adolescent girl. In China anybody older was married. They decided they could solve their problem by calling the unmarried missionaries, teachers. So the new students, unable to pronounce a word in Chinese, were immediately promoted to the rank of teachers.

As John and Zenobia walked back to their compound later that day, they laughed until tears filled their eyes at each other's efforts. Then both confessed doubt that they could ever learn the difficult language.

"But we've got to," John said. "It's going to be the key to our work here, Zenobia. We've got to learn the language and the customs. If we can do that, we can share the good news in Christ."

Resolve had replaced fear by the time they arrived at their compound.

A compound was a Chinese invention readily adopted by Western missionaries. Houses grouped close together were surrounded by a high wall for protection from marauders and robbers. In a mission compound there were usually buildings for mission activities and houses for the missionaries and their Chinese helpers.

The Connelys directed a boys' school and a girls' school in their compound, but shortly after John and Zenobia began boarding there, it was time for the Connelys to go on furlough. Senior missionaries from the China Direct Mission agreed to assume responsibility for the schools. Before either one of them could speak a decent sentence in Chinese, John Abernathy was appointed principal fo the boys' school and Zenobia Leonard was appointed principal of the girls' school.

The new missionaries had to get used to many things—customs, food, the ever-present threat of marauding warlords. Following the overthrow of the Manchus by Sun Yat-sen in 1911, China was for a time at the mercy of numerous grabs for power, none of them successful.

Many observers held that Chinese inherited a violent approach to governmental change. Historically, a new dynasty was born by overthrowing a corrupt one. After a period of time, the new dynasty would fall into corrupt patterns and would in turn be overthrown. The oldest dynasty of which there is much history, the Shang Dynasty, was challenged by Wu Wang, first ruler of the Chou Dynasty. He declared, "The iniquity of Shang is full. Heaven commands me to destroy it."

Wu Wang overthrew the Shang Dynasty and executed the king and his concubines by cutting off their heads.

Over against this violence stood the influence of Confucius, increasingly benign and impotent, however, before the plight of the common people, the great teacher's original concern. Confucius, who lived from 551 to 479 B.C., defined government as a problem in ethics. Although honored by the men of government who followed him, none seemed to incorporate his philosophy in their conduct of government.

Early in their studies the young missionaries were introduced to Confucian thought and taken on a trip to his holy mountain located nearby. Its six thousand steps were worn deep by Chinese pilgrims in search of enlightenment. The new missionaries were taken also to Chufu, Confucius's home. They made the trip Chinese style. The women were mounted on wheelbarrows which were giant wheels with side panels on which the passengers were perched to balance one another. The trip went well until they reached the normally shallow Wong River. It was swollen with the rains and the wheelbarrows could not cross. As the women tried to figure out what to do, the coolies simply waded into the river, backed up to the bank, and urged the women to climb on their backs. In the U.S.A. it was called "piggy back." In China it was called a necessity.

The Chinese teacher who accompanied the young missionaries to the shrine spoke eloquently concerning the virtues of Confucius. He concluded by saying, "I feel sure Confucius would have been a disciple of Jesus had he known him, for Confucius was a lover of truth."

It was a good thought, but John was skeptical.

He and Zenobia talked at length about Confucian thought.

"But he missed it, Zenobia. He said all men are good, and he was wrong. He had only to look around him," John said. "Only Christ can make men good."

The two young missionaries studied in Taian for two years. The full days passed fast. One reason was the principal's roles they carried in addition to their studies even after the Connelys returned.

The time came to develop a high school for the progressing students. Because of money limitations, they recommended a "co-ed" school—a new idea in China. To everyone's surprise it worked. Fierce competition between the men and women spurred both groups to new learning heights.

John, whose first love was preaching and field evangelism, relished itinerate preaching in the countryside. Again and again he risked robbers and foraging troops of competing warlords to preach in the rural churches. Sometimes he traveled by train, sometimes by ricksha, often by donkey, and very often on foot. He stayed in Chinese homes, eating Chinese food and learning Chinese customs the hard way. By 1924 he was very much at home in such circumstances.

Often while traveling he climbed a hill side to rest and think. In his mind he was nurturing a plan. He did not intend to be the mission's most eligible bachelor all his life. There had been girl friends back in North Carolina and at the seminary in Fort Worth. They were attractive and he enjoyed their company. But he had not let himself get serious because he was going to China and he did not know what to expect. How could he ask someone to face that kind of unknown? He had decided that only after he learned the culture and the language and knew what to expect would he return to North Carolina to find a wife. He could prepare her for what they would face, and together they would journey back to China to spend their lives sharing the gospel.

The term of service for most missionaries, including those of the China Direct Mission, was seven years. In the fall of 1924 John was over halfway through his first term.

At times he thought of the unmarried missionaries in the area. Any one of the young women would make a fine companion. And, of course, there was Zenobia, his friend with the big grin and the bright eyes and the strong voice.

Once, they accompanied the Connelys on a weekend Bible-teaching mission. The men stayed in the front court of their host's home and taught the men. The missionary women went into the back court to teach the Chinese women. Both groups sang.

The men could hear the women singing. One of the Chinese men turned to John and said, "I did not know the women had an organ."

John replied, "They don't."

They listened again. Then John laughed and said, "That's Miss Leonard. She has a rather strong voice."

A mate was not all that was on John's mind. The North China Mission of the Southern Baptist Foreign Mission Board had invited him to join that Mission. John had to admit he had often wished he were related to the strong Southern Baptist Mission. He liked the fellowship and he liked the firm base support emanating from the churches back home. Money worries were a problem with the China Direct Mission. Disbursement of funds received from home often brought tensions.

He took a vacation to talk to some of the Southern Baptist missionaries about the matter.

In 1900 there were only 49 Southern Baptist missionaries in all of China. By 1924 there were 287. The North China Mission first asked John to consider a position in Pingtu, the village where the storied Lottie Moon had worked. But he could not feel right about it. Next they asked him to go to Tsinan (Gee-nan), the capital of Shantung. He decided he would talk to Zenobia Leonard about his decision as soon as he returned to Taian.

As John walked into the girl's school in Taian on the Monday of his return, one of the Chinese students walked by bowing and smiling.

John asked, "Is the principal in?"

"Oh, yes, the principal is in," the student said, again bowing and smiling.

John walked to the door, opened it, and said, "Hey, I need some advice."

Then he stopped. Turning to him was Bertha Brevard.

"Hi, what can I do for you?" she asked.

She was the new principal.

While John Abernathy was preaching and reflecting in the interior, Zenobia Leonard had undergone a soul-searching of her own. At the close of the semester bedlam reigned. The girls of her school ripped up their straw mattresses and scattered the straw over their rooms. As Zenobia had learned, it was not rebellion but custom. Yet, it was a custom she was not prepared to accept, just as she had not been prepared to accept the custom of binding girls' feet.

Zenobia had enforced the rule that girls with bound feet could not matriculate. To go to school or to bind their feet was a difficult decision for some of the young girls. Without bound feet they would not fit the traditional concept of Chinese beauty and that might limit possibilities for a "good" marriage. But Zenobia was sure she was on firm ground. The crippling effects of this ancient tradition could not be justified under any circumstances.

And yet as she viewed the strewn straw, something went out of Zenobia. She prayed earnestly that night, "Lord, is this what you want me to do?"

She had never really questioned her work before. Now more and more she found herself wanting to get out into the villages to teach illiterate Chinese women to read their own language. She knew this would give her an opportunity to win them to Christ. Zenobia believed the drab life of Chinese women, who were too often dismissed as stupid and unteachable, could be reversed through the gospel. She was impressed by the example of another Baptist missionary, Miss Blanche Walker, who had developed some excellent methods for teaching illiterate women to read.

She wished she could talk with John about it, but he wasn't there. Besides, she reminded herself, John didn't bring her to China; the Lord did.

In the throes of her restlessness, Bertha Brevard, who had been working in another station since the early days of language school, came for a visit. Bertha had been one of the Direct Mission group who came with John and Zenobia. They talked long into the night bringing each other up to date.

As Bertha told her of her dream to open a school, Zenobia grew pensive.

"I really am convinced that this is what the Lord wants me to do," Bertha said with a great sense of confidence.

It was as if somebody turned on a light in Zenobia's mind. More than anything else, what had dampened her dreams to go to the interior to teach women was the realization there was no one to take her job in Taian.

She grabbed Bertha's hand, "How would you like to have a school ready made?"

Bertha looked puzzled. "Where?" she asked.

"Here," Zenobia replied.

As they talked on, the two women decided that this was why the Lord had brought them together. They soon arranged with their senior missionaries to swap jobs and stations. When John returned, Miss Brevard was principal of the girls' school and Zenobia Leonard was the only American in a remote station called Tawenkow thirty miles away.

In Tawenkow, Zenobia found new zest in her work. The Chinese women accepted her and seemed to love her. Early one evening as she sat close to a charcoal brazier keeping warm, there was a knock on the door. She went to it to find one of the Chinese women who was attending her Bible class.

"Teacher, would you mind if I slept in front of your door tonight?"

Zenobia looked puzzled. "Please come in," she invited. "It's very cold out there. Why would you want to sleep in front of my door when you have a warm house?"

"Teacher, there are many, many bad men in the area, and I will be much safer if I sleep in front of your door."

The Chinese women knew Zenobia depended on the Lord. They assumed the Lord would protect her and them if they were with her. Patiently Zenobia explained to the woman that the Lord would protect her wherever she was if she would ask and trust him. When the woman left to go back to her own house, Zenobia returned to the brazier with a good feeling. Not even the news that bandits were raping and plundering in the area robbed her of the confidence the women expressed in her.

Teaching a group to read was not as easy as it sounded.

Written Chinese, unlike most other languages, has no alphabet. English has twenty-six letters in its alphabet, but Chinese has a different character for each word. A person who wishes to read Chinese must master thousands of symbols that at times seem arbitrary and unrelated. Zenobia found out, however, after four years of patient effort, that the characters are not really arbitrary. Many words for objects can be recognized as pictures of those objects. The Chinese went through some rather complex rationalizations to arrive at particular sounds. For instance, the picture of a musical instrument came to mean "to take pleasure in" and finally evolved into "pleasure."

For Zenobia, the joy of seeing the Chinese women learn to read God's Word more than offset the difficulties. The teaching process accelerated her own progress in mastering the language. Of course, some words still puzzled her, and she was still misunderstood at times; but her ability to laugh at herself and to accept in good grace the laughter of the Chinese people kept her going.

Zenobia's days in Tawenkow were not without a degree of loneliness. She missed fellowship in her own language and easy access to friends. Most of all, she missed her talks with John Abernathy. He had written of his opportunity to align himself with the Southern Baptist Foreign Mission Board and she prayed daily for his decision.

Early in December John wrote Zenobia that he had accepted the invitation of the Foreign Mission Board and been assigned to Tsinan. He would be principal of the boys' school there and do evangelistic work in the area. While Zenobia was aware of the growing number of friendships John had among Southern Baptist missionaries, she knew it was a decision he had made in prayer.

As the winter intensified, she sat closer to her charcoal brazier at the end of the day and thought about John. He had told her how he had learned to trust the Lord for every need. It was the experience of having God answer his prayers for every need and especially his financial need that had helped to draw him to the faith approach of the China Direct Mission.

Later he had said to her, "I've learned that being a faith missionary has to do with much more than the way you receive your financial support."

There were some problems in Zenobia's mind about her relationship to the China Direct Mission, but that's where God had led her, and that's where she would stay.

In December 1924, John Arch Abernathy moved to Tsinan as a Southern Baptist mission. He arrived just before Christmas at the Baptist compound where the J. V. Daweses lived and spent the holiday with these delightful people, sharing their gracious hospitality. He learned that they were having to leave China due to Mrs. Dawes's frail health. But they hoped to stay on until June in order to help John adjust to his new responsibility. Their house would be his when they left. Meanwhile, he would live in a smaller house on the compound.

As Mrs. Dawes showed him through the house, she said, "We're not going to try to take all this furniture, so I'll be giving some of it away. I want you to take some of it."

John thanked her for her graciousness. He liked these people and regretted their leaving.

"And you know who would enjoy several of these pieces?" Mrs. Dawes continued.

"No. Who?" John asked.

"Zenobia Leonard. I know she must be living in less than comfortable circumstances down at Tawenkow. Some pieces of this furniture should help. I'll write and ask her to come by to pick them up in the spring."

John said nothing, but the thought of the friend he had not seen since her departure from Taian quickened his sense of loss. He enjoyed the company of the other missionary women, married and single, but he missed Zenobia.

"Why did I feel so comfortable with her?" he wondered.

At year's end John reviewed the eventful months. Five years ago, he reminded himself, he had been in Fort Worth at Southwestern Seminary soaking up the teaching of its able professors and the friendship of fellow students like Charlie Culpepper. Charlie and his wife should be coming to China very soon under the auspices of the Southern Baptist Convention. It would be good to have them as fellow missionaries. There was even a possibility they would be assigned to Shantung Province.

John also thought about home. His mother had died early in the year and there had been very little contact with his brothers and sisters, though he had written some. He had looked forward to furlough when he would see her again. The realization that she would not be there hurt.

He continued to worry about China's political fortunes. Something called communism had appeared in 1921, the year after he arrived in Shanghai. Imported from Russia, it nevertheless flourished in China. Toward the end of the year, because of alliances between Sun Yat-sen and the Russians, the National People's Party of the Kuomintang had followed the Communists to become members. Perhaps the Communist movement ought not to worry him, but its avowedly atheistic position did bother John. He prayed that Sun Yat-sen and his young protegé, Chiang Kai-shek, could master the problems of unifying China before the Communists grew strong enough to do so.

Although the American newspapers and magazines to which he subscribed came late and the letters received were few, he kept up with what was happening over the world. He knew U. S. troops had landed in Honduras. He knew a man named Adolph Hitler had been sentenced to prison in Europe, and he attached little significance to it. The post-war European scene was pretty unstable, he decided.

Calvin Coolidge, a Republican, had been elected President of the United States. This disturbed his Democratic blood, but as the Bible admonished, he prayed for Coolidge even as he prayed for Sun Yat-sen and Chiang Kai-shek.

Lack of information about the 1924 Olympics in Paris frustrated John and reminded him that four years had passed since he left the United States. The last Olympic Games had been held just before he came to China.

John knew that Nicolai Lenin, so instrumental in the Russian Communist revolution, had died, as had America's beloved Woodrow Wilson.

John continued to keep a wary eye on Japan, for Japan made increasing demands on China and looked more and more militaristic. Japanese troops were already in Shantung Province under a variety of excuses, and the Chinese were not strong enough to object. As he encountered the posturing aggressiveness of Japanese militants in the streets of Tsinan, he had an uneasy feeling.

As 1925 began, John dug into his new work. His experience as principal of the boys' school in Taian served him well in similar responsibilities in Tsinan. The faculty and students responded to his leadership, his grasp of Chinese, his growing understanding of the culture, and his obvious love for them. The Daweses marveled at the way he got into the work and the energy with which he addressed it. In addition to his school responsibilities, he moved in and out of the churches in Tsinan and in surrounding villages, preaching and teaching with great enthusiasm. At times he worried about the lack of response, as well as the lack of commitment of some of the Chinese Christian leaders. He wondered why his own preaching was not more effective. His natural optimism remained high, however, and his commitment was strong. He could leave the results to the Lord.

In May he went by to help the Daweses pack.

"Hi, John. Guess who's coming to visit us," Mrs. Dawes said.

"Who?" John asked.

"Zenobia Leonard. She'll be here tonight. You've got to have dinner with us tomorrow."

"I'll do it," John said.

As he went back to the school, his step lightened with excitement.

John Abernathy was elated to know that Zenobia Leonard was to visit Tsinan. His mind had been preoccupied with thoughts of her. He had become obsessed with those thoughts one night a few weeks before that he had resolved to write the next morning and ask her to marry him. The decision had allowed him to sleep; he dreamed of her, and it seemed that she was there. But when morning came, he found himself with cold feet, and not just from the coolness of the early dawn.

Zenobia was due to arrive at the Daweses' home that evening. He decided to go by to see if she wanted to go with him the next day to the university where he was to speak. Afterward, he would approach the subject of marriage. God willing, he would do just that.

Zenobia Leonard tried to contain her own excitement as she unpacked in the guest room of the Daweses' house. Mrs. Dawes had been thoughtful to invite her, and the pieces of furniture that were to be hers were beautiful. She had already made arrangements to get them to Tawenkow. Now she could look forward to the fellowship. It would be especially good to see John Abernathy. She wondered if he had found somebody else to take her place as friend and confidante. Probably, she thought to herself as she unfolded a dress to hang in the wardrobe. After all, John got along with everybody.

She enjoyed her work in Tawenkow and felt very much in God's will as she understood it. When she was lonely for American companionship, she treated it as a call to prayer. Now for a few days she would have companionship and she would enjoy it.

There was a knock on the door.

"Yes," she called.

It was Mrs. Dawes. "There's someone here to see you, Zenobia," she said. "Can you come down?"

"Yes," Zenobia replied. "I'm almost through unpacking. I'll be right down."

As Zenobia came down the steps, she saw John standing at the bottom. He was grinning broadly.

"Zenobia, you're a sight for sore eyes," he said.

They chatted briefly before John asked her if she would like to go with him to the university. Then they talked animatedly all the way to the university and back. She was profuse in her compliments of his message. When they reached the compound, John risked a breach of etiquette and asked her to come into his cottage to see his new guitar. To his relief, she agreed.

Inside, Zenobia sat demurely on the divan as John picked up his guitar and said, "Let me sing for you."

He sang "Spanish Cavalier" strongly, with only a little bit of embarrassment. She was delighted, and her face showed it. He relaxed.

John quickly put the guitar to one side and leaned across towards her. "Zenobia, that's not the real reason I wanted you to come in. The real reason is that I love you and I want you to marry me."

John reported later that his heart was "pounding like a loaded locomotive pulling a heavy train up a mountain."

Zenobia caught her breath for a moment. But she knew there was no need to be coy or to think this one through.

Her voice was warm and her eyes moist as she said softly, "I never cared for anyone as I do for you, John."

It was a natural response for Zenobia. The feelings she had for John when she first saw him on the train in Kansas City almost five years before; the admiration, the friendship, the respect during the months of language school; the responsibilities they shared in the Taian schools and the long talks whenever they were together all added up. She loved him.

They had never had a date. Such would have been unthinkable in China. But the times they had together were a treasure of memories nurtured in lonely moments.

Before Zenobia had a chance to say more, John said eagerly, "Well, could we get married next week?"

His smile was irresistible.

She laughed, "No. I can't get ready in a week."

"All right. How about June? The missionaries will be going to Mission meeting in Chefoo, and they can all stop off for our wedding."

Again she laughed. "I can be ready by then. That will be fine."

The two clasped hands, still too shy and too uncertain to do more. Then they rushed to tell the Daweses. The older couple, feeling like very successful matchmakers, were delighted.

That night as they gathered around the table, Mr. Dawes offered thanks with a glad voice and asked rich blessings for John and Zenobia.

After the prayer, John said, "Did you know that Zenobia's middle name is Jewell?" He looked at Zenobia. "Now she's my jewel, and that's what I'm going to call her."

Jewell beamed.

Later when John returned to his cottage, he told his housekeeper Brother Pea, "I've a secret to tell you, my friend, but you must not tell anybody."

Brother Pea's face brightened. "Oh, I will not tell anyone."

"I'm engaged to be married!"

Brother Pea could not contain his enthusiasm. He hopped around the room with gladness. The shame and waste of this fine young man living by himself would soon be over. The terrible situation of that fine young woman living by herself would cease.

"Of course," he said, "I'm not at all surprised. We have known for a long time that you and Miss Leonard would one day marry."

"How did you know?" John asked.

Brother Pea just smiled. Some things were too hard to explain to a Westerner.

Both young missionaries wrote home, though they doubted whether the letters would reach their families and friends before the wedding ceremony. Zenobia—now Jewell to all—wished her father could be there. But this was where God had brought her, and this the man to whom God had led her. Therefore, this was the way it would be.

John dutifully wrote Mr. Leonard asking for Jewell's hand in marriage. Although the letter could not get there before the ceremony it seemed the right thing to do.

Preparations for the wedding went smoothly. John and Jewell asked Mr. Blalock, the man who brought them to China under the China Direct Mission, to perform their marriage ceremony. They both shed tears of appreciation when the Daweses, who would have to leave before the wedding, presented them their dining room furniture as a wedding gift. By visit and by letter they selected a wedding party. A missionary friend of Jewell's, Maxine McNeal, would be the maid of honor. Bertha Brevard would sing. A Methodist couple, the Leitzels, would play the instruments. A missionary named Fred Pike was asked to be John's best man and two missionary children, Ann Lois Baker and Ruthie Pike, agreed to be flower girls. The Frank Connely's four-year-old son Billy would be the ring-bearer. Missionaries and Chinese friends from both stations volunteered a host of other services.

The wedding would be at Taian since it was the place they both lived most of their time in China and would be on the way to Chefoo for many of the Southern Baptist missionaries going to Mission meeting.

At the last minute John and Jewell were persuaded to have a honeymoon. They had originally planned to go directly from Taian to the Dawes home in Tsinan to take up housekeeping. But friends in the Methodist compound said it would be a shame for them not to have at least two or three days in Tai Shan, Confucius's sacred mountain, where there were a number of vacation cottages. They insisted that John and Jewell let them prepare a cottage for them.

John and Jewell were married at two o'clock in the afternoon. It was a family-like affair for the missionaries who attended. A wedding on the field was not a new thing for the missionaries, but it happened seldom enough to provide a memorable social affair.

The Frank Connelys had brought a Model-T Ford to China when they returned from furlough. Jewell Leonard Abernathy, at three o'clock in the afternoon of June 20, 1925, became the first bride ever to ride through the city of Taian in an automobile.

When they could go no further in the Model-T Ford, John rented two mountain chairs to take them the rest of the way up the mountain. The scenery was breathtaking. They arrived in time to watch a magnificent sunset. John held Jewell close as he recited Psalm 19:1, "The heavens declare the glory of God, and the firmament showeth his handiwork."

That night by their marriage bed, they quoted Matthew 19:5, "For this cause shall a man leave father and mother, and shall cleave to his wife: and they twain shall be one flesh."

3
Shantung Revival

When John and Jewell Abernathy moved into the Dawes home in Tsinan the summer of 1925, China was a complicated mixture of things that refused to change and things that changed at a dizzying pace. The things that refused to change seemed to flow around the Chinese life-style—home, family, peasantry, and suffering from the ravages of nature—ravages such as famine and flooding.

The things that changed most rapidly seemed to revolve around politics and the quest for power.

In March, Sun Yat-sen had died of cancer, and his young military aide, Chiang Kai-shek, though ostensibly sharing Sun's mantle, had increasingly taken over the leadership of the Kuomintang. A few days before John and Jewell's wedding an incident occurred which increased the pace of political change.

A group of British soldiers fired upon Chinese students and workers who were demonstrating in a textile strike. Twelve were killed and many more wounded. Like America's Boston Massacre, the incident galvanized Chinese resistance to foreign intervention and increased the desire for a unified government. That incident, followed by others later in the summer, precipitated a wave of antiforeign acts.

In the interior, missionaries were harrassed and sometimes forced to flee for their lives. Reactionary Chinese leaders declared the missionary's presence an insult—despite their good works—because it represented an affront to ancient Chinese traditions.

The Kuomintang found the turmoil favorable to its aspirations, and in the month after John and Jewell were married, the Kuomintang proclaimed itself the Nationalist Government of China.

John and Jewell stayed abreast of such events, but they were not politically preoccupied. Yet, the realities of battle, strikes, shortages, and rumors sweeping back and forth through Shantung affected the school they served and also their evangelistic work in outlying areas.

In 1926 the Abernathys were a part of nearly eight thousand Protestant missionaries and probably four thousand Catholic missionaries in China. For the most part, missionaries supported by liberal foreign journals identified the Kuomintang and Chiang Kai-shek with the American Revolution and George Washington. More conservative portions of the American press and government were not sure.

As Chiang Kai-shek moved to take Shanghai, United States marines were sent in to boost the American military garrison. The American commandant said he was not there to oppose the Chinese Nationalists, but only to protect American lives in China. The American consul advised Americans in Tsinan to leave.

Missionaries gathered in individual homes to consider the situation. Some thought there was a strong Communist element in the Kuomintang because of the presence of Red Army advisers resulting from agreements Sun Yat-sen made with the Russians before he died. Some missionaries felt communism might be a source of potential reform for China's age-old problems, but John Abernathy disagreed. He had a deep distrust of anything communistic, though he trusted Chiang Kai-shek. However, he tried to keep his concerns local and his life centered on his calling. He was not in China to preach politics or nationalism; he was there for Christ and it was men's souls he was concerned about.

And, despite the periodic distractions brought about by political changes, economic ups and downs, natural disasters, and war, the work in Tsinan continued. Besides being principal of the Chungchoong Boys School in Tsinan, the Mission assigned John to a five-county field in the Shantung Province that bracketed China's famed Yellow River.

As soon as school was out, John prepared to take his new wife into the field with him. He hired a ricksha to pick her up at home and take her the first fifty *li* (approximately sixteen miles). His economy-minded bride suggested that instead they go to the ricksha stand because they should be able to strike a better deal there. But John felt it would be better to have the ricksha pick her up at the house. For Jewell this was a problem. A lot of Zenobia, the single missionary, was still there.

One of the weaknesses she discovered in herself when she first arrived in China was the habit of depending on her father for decision-making. Determined to overcome this dependence, she quickly learned to make firm decisions and rely on them confidently. Now what should she do when she thought one thing and her husband thought another?

Well, the Bible was clear, she felt. When she accepted John as her husband, she accepted him as the head of their house. She didn't intend to check her brains at the gate, but she did intend to learn to follow him.

The wisdom of his choice in the matter was soon evident. The deference the ricksha driver gave to a lady picked up at her home contrasted sharply with the kind of ride she would receive from the low bidder at a ricksha stand. And the price was not too different either.

With John on a bicycle leading the way, they rolled out into the countryside. The howling North China wind was punishing to the American missionaries. Apparently, the stoical Chinese pulling the ricksha in a trot he seemingly could maintain all day was not bothered.

Jewell wrapped herself tightly in a blanket, pulling close to her side a woven bamboo basket. It contained some Chinese tracts, a Chinese Bible, and two hundred Chinese pennies to be used in the rural area for favors and food.

The wind became so punishing to John that he rode ahead to seek shelter where he could await the ricksha.

As the ricksha approached a small village, Jewell was settled in her blanket like a cocoon in a shell. Ahead, she would see John crouched in the lee of the village wall awaiting for their arrival. Suddenly, at a low place in the road the coolie stumbled and over the richsha went. John came running as he saw his bride tumble out of the ricksha and roll into a ditch.

To the delight of the ever-present Chinese children, pennies and tracts from the basket scattered everywhere. They began to scramble for the pennies, keeping a wary eye on Jewell. She untangled herself from her blanket, sat upright, and looked around. As she took in the scene, she began to laugh uproariously. The children stopped to watch her, and then they began to laugh. Soon, instead of grabbing pennies and running, they gathered them and enthusiastically returned them to Jewell. John was amazed.

Chinese friends with whom they stayed and to whom John delight-edly introduced his new bride added to his assurance. They were glad John had found a wife for they had been afraid he would be unable to. One old gentleman confided to Jewell that he had assumed John was too poor to afford one. Appraising Jewell's round-eyed grin, he suggested John might be richer than he thought. Jewell bowed, said all the proper things, and prayed she would not break up with laughter.

The second part of their trip took them across the Yellow River. Fortunately, the strong winds of the first part had subsided. Winds made the Hwang Ho, as the Yellow River was called by the Chinese, treacherous to cross. The boatman employed to take them across the river moved his boat with a long pole. As the boatman poled, the Chinese boy who was his helper talked incessantly to the missionaries. Jewell watched the boatman intently. Suddenly he pulled the pole up, laid it aside, and picked up an oar. As he did so the boy sang out, "The ocean may have a bottom, but the Hwang Ho does not."

Later, the boatman laid aside the oar and picked up the pole. The boy again sang out, "The bottom has returned."

As they crossed, the boy regaled the Abernathys with stories of the fury, capriciousness, and greatness of the Yellow River. The newlyweds enjoyed him tremendously.

The third part of the trip necessitated still another form of trans-portation. This time John rented two donkeys. To Jewell they seemed little larger than the jack rabbits back home in Arkansas.

There was neither saddle nor stirrup. John threw their bedrolls across the donkeys' backs for saddles. Then the Chinese man who rented the beasts to them crouched nearby, pointing to his knee. After a moment Jewell understood she was to put her foot on the man's knee and climb onto the donkey's back. It seemed easy enough. She mounted without difficulty, but it turned out to be a very temporary situation. To the donkey owner's consternation, John's cry of alarm, and the children's delight, she slid off the animal's back, landing very unceremoniously on that part of her own anatomy.

Jewell laughed, the donkey man grinned nervously, and even John tried to smile. The second time was a repeat of the first without the laughs. John told the donkey man he needed a larger animal. The donkey man said the donkey was trying to bluff her. He pled with John: "If this donkey gets away with this, I will never be able to use it again. You must help me."

The third try worked. But when Jewell dismounted from her pint-sized steed that evening, she felt she could never walk again.

One night in 1926, John and Jewell were awakened by bearers of the news that the American vice-president of Nanking University had been killed during a terrorist uprising. National troops rampaging through the city had killed six foreigners.

Pearl Buck, the famous author, had to take refuge along with her children in a Chinese home. She wrote, "The whirlwinds were gathering . . . and I was reaping where I had not sown. . . . We were hiding for our lives because we were white."

As a result of the uprising, John and Jewell and other missionaries came under new pressure to flee to one of the treaty ports for safety. Approximately 2,500 missionaries took refuge in Shanghai. Over 5,000 left the country. Many missionary schools, colleges, and hospitals were closed or taken over by the Nationalists.

John stubbornly refused to leave. If his own resolve was not enough, his independently minded wife—his Jewell—was additional support.

"If we ran every time we heard a rumor," she maintained, "running would be our full-time work."

John had great confidence in the American marines. If things got too rough, he felt sure the 4,000 "leathernecks" in Tientsin, equipped with their 20 airplanes and their light tanks, could whisk them safely away.

Thus, the Abernathys continued to work in Chinese homes and in outlying areas, evangelizing and strengthening the churches. It was hard work and political uncertainty complicated it.

For a time the Nationalists were unable to push their control beyond Nanking. Shantung in 1927 was controlled by an earthy warlord nearly seven feet tall. Chang Tsung-chang was said to keep 42 concubines, including one American, on his own private railroad train. In the ultimate tradition of warlords, he was a despot, and under his debauched leadership Shantung was plagued by corruption and disorder. Chang controlled a group of Russian cavalry which rampaged through the countryside and provoked a retaliatory group called the Red Spears. Made up of rural Chinese organized to defend themselves, the Red Spears responded with cruelty, dispatch, and very little discrimination.

These two groups, along with the century-old robber bands that roamed the province, made John's sorties into the countryside risky, to say the least. A famine that plagued Shantung that year and the next made the robbers even bolder, but John's concern for the Chinese common man, who was called "Old Hundred Names," did not allow him to rest in the relative safety of Tsinan.

The latter part of 1927 John and Jewell returned to the United States for their first furlough. The changes in their own country were marked. Henry Ford's product was everywhere they looked. Opulent new homes were going up. Radio was ubiquitous. The big-band music of the furious '20s permeated every part of their native land. The scars of a nation trying to recover from World War I were gone, covered over by the excitement of unparalleled prosperity.

Some of their friends were buying stocks and watching them double in a matter of weeks. Some were borrowing money and purchasing items that only the rich could afford when they left the States. The days of Ben Franklin were abandoned with all the enlightened assurance that only the materially sophisticated can muster.

John wasn't sure about it all. Jewell was. America had given itself over to a materialistic temptation that was sure to boomerang.

The excitement of being home and renewing acquaintance with loved ones and friends offset their reverse cultural shock, however.

They went first to Arkansas to visit Jewell's family. For her it was an emotional reunion with her father and his second wife and her younger brothers and sisters. They gathered on the porch to listen to Jewell tell of China and they thronged around her handsome young groom with curiosity and growing affection. John was an immediate hit. Mr. Leonard said he had known when he first met John on the train in Kansas City that he was a fine young man.

The missionaries visited neighbors and former teachers. John preached in Jewell's home church and in nearby churches with which she had kept faithful contact during their time in China. That was a habit born when they were "faith" missionaries and depended on those contracts for support. Jewell figured it was just as important to keep contact when they were supported by a Board as it had been before. The prayer support was even more critical than the money.

Just before coming home, Jewell had received appointment by the Foreign Mission Board. It was only because John had already been appointed, for the Board did not have money to send any new missionaries at that time.

Southern Baptists' Seventy-five Million Campaign, which included the "call out the called" emphasis that had been used to reach Zenobia Jewell Leonard, had developed a backlash. While over $90,000,000 was pledged throughout the Convention and allocated to various agencies including the Foreign Mission Board, only $54,000,000 had been collected. The Boards, hoping for the pledge amount, had spent accordingly. Thus, while the United States was in an orgy of growing affluence, the Foreign Mission Board in Richmond was in deep debt.

After a visit to John's brothers and sisters in North Carolina, the Abernathys moved to New Orleans. John enrolled in the Baptist Theological Seminary there. (It was then called Baptist Bible Institute.) He wanted to complete work for his theological degree, for he had felt keenly his lack of a diploma while he was in China. Many of the missionaries in China had college, seminary, and even Ph.D. degrees. Although he had noted privately that not all of these men were effective workers, he coveted more training.

John studied hard during the week and on weekends spoke in churches in the area. Sometimes he and Jewell took the train to Arkansas, where they were becoming well known.

Despite America's preoccupation with her newfound affluence, there was a growing interest in China. The return of so many missionaries distressed those who had seen such promise among China's millions for the Christian faith. John tried to convince people that the missionaries primarily interested in evangelism were "hanging tight," that someday a great ingathering would come.

Privately, John and Jewell admitted a growing concern about their work in China. Deadness in the Chinese churches and unfaithfulness of many Chinese leaders were discouraging. The difficulties and uncertainties of the war raging around Shantung were taking a severe toll. Just before leaving China for furlough, Jewell had joined a group dedicated to prayer for revival.

As the time neared for their return to China, the Abernathys received word that the Board had money for their passage. They packed their barrels and trunks. Their freight included a new Model-A Ford.

When John and Jewell told fellow students about their experiences with donkeys on field trips in Shantung, the mission band at the theological school resolved to collect money to buy a car for them. Soon there was nearly enough money and the Abernathys began to realize that what they thought to be a gesture was indeed going to become a real car. The problem of shipping a car and paying the freight bill was solved quite unexpectedly. Just before they were to leave for China, friends from North Carolina surprised them with a blue Model-A Ford. The Abernathys were flabbergasted. What would they tell the students who were about ready to buy a car for them? They drove the blue car to the seminary and the students responded beautifully.

"Our money will pay the freight," they said.

"The Lord sure knows how to make things work together," John said gratefully.

The voyage back to China in 1928 was a welcome relief from the hectic pace of their year at home, and leave-taking was not as hard as it was the first time. After all, they had each other now. A few friends expressed concern that they had no children, but John and Jewell showed no concern. They were both active missionaries. Perhaps the fact they had no children was simply God's way of freeing them both to do the work he had called them to do.

As they prepared to return to China, Nationalist troops moved into Tsinan. This produced a new threat. The Japanese felt a proprietary concern for Shantung and threatened to intervene if the Nationalists did not leave Tsinan. U.S. Colonel Joseph Stilwell, who had gone to China the same year as the Abernathys and who was commander of an American military detachment in Tientsin, predicted that the Japanese could take the province easily whenever they were ready.

The month John and Jewell arrived in Tsinan and took up housekeeping once more in the house in which they had begun life together, the Nationalists completed their somewhat shakey takeover of the North and renamed Peking, Peiping, or "northern peace." It was the third major regime under which the Abernathys had lived. John shrugged it off. That was the way it was in China. He was more concerned about other things.

In 1929 the Abernathys learned that depression had struck the United States. The stock market had crashed and a disillusioned people struggled to rearrange their priorities. The heady opulence which John and Jewell had watched with awe and perplexity during their furlough had collapsed. As they read the newspapers from the States, they pondered the spiritual implications.

As soon as possible John began visiting on the field to see about the churches. To his dismay, he found that they had declined severely. Many small congregations had grown inactive. Some members had returned to idolatrous ways. Leaders had fallen into immorality. Again and again John came home from a trip to sit down heavily and say to an inquiring Jewell, "I guess I have been bearing a lot of fruit here, Jewell. At least, it looks like I am the one that's been bearing it, since it seems to fall off so easily."

Jewell was equally concerned. The groups with which she and John met to pray for revival seemed mocked by what they saw throughout 1929 and 1930. The effects of depression spread in the United States. Missionaries on furlough in the States were not able to return to the field. Budgets were trimmed further. Word came from the Board that if something didn't change, the missionaries would have to be brought home.

The spiritual hunger among the missionaries grew.

John and Jewell admitted that their own ministries seemed to lack power. Jewell's prayer group intensified its efforts, and John experienced a deepening personal frustration.

At a Bible conference in Tsinan in 1930 the great missionary Jonathan Goforth lectured on Acts 1:8, "After that ye shall receive power . . ."

The legendary missionary whose body bore the marks of his faithfulness to the Lord Christ during the terror-filled days of the Boxer Rebellion had an aura of spiritual strength. The missionaries who heard him knew they needed the same thing.

Later that year a petite Norwegian Evangelical Lutheran missionary named Marie Monsen came to Shantung. The intense little woman preached with great zeal and laid upon the hearts of the missionaries and their Chinese workers the need to claim God's promises and to stand firmly on them. She predicted that revival was coming to Shantung.

"How do you know?" Jewell queried.

"Because you have fulfilled all the conditions in 2 Chronicles 7:14," she said. "If my people, which are called by my name, shall humble themselves, and pray, and seek my face, and turn from their wicked ways; then will I hear from heaven, and will forgive their sin, and will heal their land."

Enroute to Shantung to speak to the missionaries, Miss Monsen traveled on a large steamer. Hearing shots early one morning while in her cabin, she realized the ship had been boarded and taken by pirates. "Immediately," she reported, "these words came to me: 'This is a trial of your faith. Fear not, Marie, for I am with thee. Be not dismayed, for I am thy God. I will strengthen thee.'"

The tiny woman who seemed to fear nothing intimidated the bandits by standing up to their every demand. They permitted her to keep her cabin and brought her food which she refused to eat. "I will have nothing to do with stolen food," she said firmly.

Another passenger, a Chinese merchant, slipped boiled eggs to her each night. These sustained her, but it left the pirates perplexed. Finally they released her, evidently glad to have this unsettling woman out of their midst.

In a way, she was equally unsettling to the missionaries as she told of what God had done in her life and the things she had experienced.

Jewell commented to John, "Listening to her, I know she has a closeness to the Father that I long for."

Miss Monsen's methods provoked deep self-examination. After she preached, she would stand at the door and ask each person exiting, "Have you been saved?"

It disturbed many that she asked the question of evangelists, preachers, and missionaries as well as of lay people. If they were satisfied about their salvation, she pressed them further. "Have you received the Holy Ghost? Have you been baptized with the Holy Spirit?"

Missionaries were still confessing their need for spiritual power a year later. The churches continued apathetic.

Then things began to change. A woman with the Baptist Mission spent the summer searching the Old and New Testament regarding the Holy Spirit. As she began to teach that fall, something dramatic happened in her life. Word spread throughout the Shantung Mission that one of their most dedicated missionaries had received the outpouring of the Holy Spirit in her life.

News of her experience deepened the resolve of missionaries like John and Jewell to have everything God had provided for them.

That fall John, traveling in the countryside, was caught in a frightening storm and sought refuge in a Buddhist temple. As he waited for the storm to subside, he looked with interest at the temple's interior, heavy with the smell and smoke of burning incense and dominated by a huge, ugly Buddha that reached from floor to ceiling.

As he looked around, a man shuffled into the room and up to the idol with a tray. A priest appeared from the darkness on the other side and began to strike a small gong with a mallet.

Each time the mallet struck the brass gong, the man with the tray bowed low before the idol. Following his oblation, he came to the door and stood near John, waiting for the storm to abate.

"What did you bring on the tray?" John asked.

"Food," the man said. "My son is near death, and I came to make a vow. If this god will heal my son, I will offer sacrifices of food."

John said, "But can this god eat food? Look, he is not eating the food."

The father turned to look, and then he turned back towards John. "This is not a god that can help you," John said. "This is a god made by man. He cannot heal your son."

As John talked, he noticed with concern that the man's sorrow evident when he entered the temple was deepening. A rolling series of thunderclaps gave the whole scene an eerie dimension.

John said, "There is a physician who is able to heal all kinds of diseases. He has healed the sick, opened the eyes of the blind, and made the deaf to hear."

The man's eyes lighted up and John, bolder, said, "He can heal your son."

The man's face saddened again. "But I have no money with which to pay. He must require much money."

Gently and as simply as he could John told him about Jesus and then added, "And there is no charge."

The man came nearer to John and looked at him intently, "Will you ask this great doctor to heal my son?"

John swallowed hard. Did he really believe God's promises? Suddenly, he felt it was a moment of truth. Laying a hand on the man's shoulder, John bowed his head and prayed earnestly for God to heal the man's son. As he prayed, John felt a surge of confidence.

In a moment the storm eased and the man hurried on his way after thanking John profusely and recovering the food he had placed before the idol. John continued on his way, sure that God had answered his prayer.

On another trip he stopped by a Taoist temple. Its walls were festooned with murals portraying gruesome punishments for disobedient wives and children. Stone mills grinding people up and bodies being penetrated by swords or boiled in hot oil were among the more palatable depictions. The scene moved John to pray that the people of China would be freed of such terror and that he and others trying to help them would have the power God had promised for the task.

Other missionaries in Shantung reported being filled with the Holy Spirit and word of it traveled over the grapevine of relationships and casual conversations. A noticeable excitement rippled among the Christians and especially among the missionaries.

John and Jewell entertained missionary travelers in their home. After supper local missionaries joined them to listen to the news brought and the stories told. Some of what was reported challenged their credulity: Paralytics walked after years of being bedridden. Blind people saw. There were even stories of the dead being raised. The biblical basis was carefully searched out. And they told themselves that Christians should not be surprised when such things happened.

Jewell was grateful for the things she heard, and she desperately wanted such an experience for herself. John was more pragmatic, but he also confessed a growing hunger for what was increasingly referred to as the "baptism of the Holy Spirit." This experience seemed to be the common denominator in the miracles reported.

The Pentecostal dimensions in the claims bothered John. Reports of individuals speaking in tongues and participating in ecstatic demonstrations of joy were rampant. But he decided such things should not deter his search.

Missionaries receiving the experience of the Holy Spirit immediately shared it with others by letter or face to face. The precipitating factor in nearly every case reported was the confession of sin and a sense of forgiveness after which God poured out his Spirit upon the forgiven sinner.

It became a frustrating thing for John and Jewell. They had confessed their sins. Jewell grew particularly intense. For several years she had built an expectancy concerning the filling of the Holy Spirit.

In 1927 when her friend, Mrs. Charles Culpepper (Sr.), experienced a dramatic healing of her eyes, Jewell became convinced God would do miraculous things in any life fully offered up to him.

She often listened to Reuben Torrey, Jr., John's good friend, talk of his father's experience, and she read the senior Torrey's book on the Holy Spirit until the pages were literally falling out.

Marie Monsen's teaching and her quiet power also remained fresh in Jewell's memory.

Yet she wanted to avoid the sin of Simon who simply wanted the blessing for the personal power it would bring. She wanted God's power in God's time for God's purposes.

Jewell's Bible study and prayer times consumed more and more time. She felt she would burst if God did not fill her.

When a fellow missionary in Tsinan, Mary Crawford, experienced a filling with the Holy Spirit, Jewell said, "John, I am so hungry for God's Spirit that I ache all over."

She wrote letters to friends confessing any sins she remembered and making restitution to the best of her ability. She read Ephesians 5:18 and prayed, "Lord, you have commanded us to be filled with your Spirit. I ask you to fill me."

She read Luke 11:13, "How much more shall your heavenly Father give the Holy Spirit to them that ask him." And she prayed. Exhausted, she asked God, "What else is there to do?"

All-night prayer meetings began, and Jewell became a dedicated participant. One night as she was praying with Mary Crawford and a small group of Chinese women, she felt the Spirit's presence in the group in a special way. Later that night several of the women went home, but three stayed. One was Jewell.

She shared her ache with the other two and said, "Pray for me," and then she began to pray. She said, "Father, I have confessed every sin I can remember. Now I am going to confess things that I am not even sure about. But I am going to call them sin too."

Suddenly, without warning, the floodgates of heaven opened. The joy that jumped up, full grown, in her heart could not be contained. She began to praise God and weep for joy. The experience grabbed her so completely she was almost ready to ask relief from it when it began to subside.

Later she slept briefly and then joined the morning prayer group at the church. Subdued, humble, and grateful, she gave her testimony. To her joy she saw the Chinese women who had sat so impassively in such services before begin to weep and pray. "Thank you, Lord," she said. "Now use me as you will."

The days that followed were like walking on air for Jewell. The humblest Christian could admonish her, and she would take it as a word from the Master. Life was totally different. John beheld all this with amazement.

In the early days of the revival John spent much time in Bible study, working his way through teachings concerning the Holy Spirit. He was especially preoccupied with the terms "baptized with the Holy Spirit," "receiving the Holy Spirit," "being filled with the Holy Spirit," and the "gift of the Holy Spirit."

"But I've always been taught that such an experience was only for Christians of the first century," John remonstrated as one of his friends shared his testimony.

"I don't know about that," the friend said. "I just know what's happened to me."

After a time John laid aside his study. He just wanted whatever God would give him. He knew the Lord had used him and that people had come to Christ under his preaching. But he also faced squarely the defeats, fears, and anxieties that had punctuated such victories.

He was impressed with those who had experienced the Spirit and who now preached with new power and resulting victories. He felt that the difference in their ministry was undeniable.

Like Jewell, John prayed regularly with Chinese friends. Several of them were in church with him one morning praying for God's blessing. Suddenly, John came face to face with an old memory. During his furlough while completing his work at Baptist Bible Institute, he arranged with professors to finish the final requirements for his degree at home in Arkansas before returning to China. One of the questions called for a biblical answer. John looked in the Bible for the Scripture passage. It seemed an innocent enough thing to do, and he had not felt guilty about the situation at the time. But now the memory smothered him. He knew it was robbing him of peace. On his knees he promised the Lord he would write a letter to the president and return his diploma.

The diploma meant more to John than he had been willing to admit. The humiliation of having to write such a letter devastated him. But no sooner had he made his promise to the Lord than "the fountains broke loose in my inmost being," he reported to Jewell. "I was cleansed and filled so full I felt as though I could not stand it."

On that same morning two Chinese pastors received the same experience, and John reported their morning together as "beyond description."

The next morning John preached in the Tsinan church. He chose the text Hosea 10:12, "Sow to yourselves in righteousness, reap in mercy; break up your fallow ground: for it is time to seek the Lord, till he come and rain righteousness upon you."

John hardly made sense, he talked so fast. His ideas bubbled up faster than he could deliver them. At the close he extended an invitation. Great numbers came forward to pray, deeply broken and convicted of sin.

John later said, "From that point on, my life and work were all in the Lord—a little instrument in his big hands."

For John the difference between preaching in his own strength and preaching under the anointing of the Spirit was as the difference between daylight and darkness.

In prayer one night the Abernathys and Mary Crawford became convinced that the Shantung experience had to be shared with the people back home. Letters were written to puzzled friends in the United States who hardly knew how to account for the sudden confession of sins, not to mention the accounts of miracles beyond belief.

Hurriedly, Mary Crawford gathered up many of these stories and arranged them in a book which was published in North China and sent back to the States in limited quantities.

The common denominator in the confession of sins seemed to be a personal humiliation. Sometimes it was a large gross sin that accounted for the humiliation, sometimes it was a sin seemingly so minor as to be laughable. Either way, the humiliation was accomplished and a contrite heart resulted. The empty vessel then received an outpouring of God's Spirit.

Many who heard what was going on in China, though puzzled by the stories of miraculous events and confession of sins, were impressed that a Mission which had only a hundred baptisms the year before the revival began had recorded three thousand baptisms in the first year it began. The North China seminary, which had only four students when the fire fell, was bursting at the seams with 125 students a year later.

A few months after his experience, John was ministering with one of the Chinese pastors who was seeking to be filled with the Holy Spirit. The man appeared at John's door one morning and confessed that they had a fellowship problem. John was shocked. He invited him in and asked, "What is it, dear friend?"

"It's your gold ring," the Chinese pastor admitted, bowing his head with the shame of his statement.

John took the ring off his finger, held it up, and said, "This is the way we signify our commitments to one another in marriage in our country. Mrs. Abernathy put this on my finger and I put one on her finger."

The pastor began to weep. "The devil keeps telling me, 'Look at his gestures. Look at how he uses his left hand. He is just showing off his gold ring.' "

John, who was left-handed, said, "If my wedding ring causes my brother to stumble, then I will discontinue the use of it. Quietly he put the ring in his pocket.

When he told Jewell about the pastor's visit, she said, "Well, you do whatever you want to, but I don't think we need to carry things that far. After all, it is a symbol of our marriage."

A few weeks later another phenomena of the revival changed Jewell's mind. A woman was brought to church services in Tsinan by a friend. The friend explained that the woman was tormented by a demon, that sometimes she would fall in the fire or foam at the mouth in torture. Christians often prayed for her, but as her friend said, "We can pray her free, but she does not stay free."

After the service, they decided to have a prayer meeting for the woman and gathered around her. The Chinese pastor leading the group said, "I think it will be necessary to remove her jewelry. She has rings on every finger and bracelets on her arm and ornaments in her hair. Some of this is superstitious jewelry dedicated to her gods. Perhaps this is the reason she is not free." Then he turned to Jewell, "Would you ask her, Mrs. Abernathy?"

Jewell consented. As she started talking to the woman, she found herself trying to hide her wedding ring. She stopped and bowed her head. It was as if God spoke to her and said, "What right do you have to ask her to remove her rings while you still have yours on?"

Jewell took her ring off. Then they prayed, and as they did, the woman was released from her bondage.

Later that night, Jewell shared the experience with John, and the two of them agreed they would sell their rings to the local goldsmith and use the money to help educate a young woman whom they had led to the Lord and who wanted to be a nurse.

John said, "Well, now, we've had two double-ring ceremonies."

During this time it was almost impossible for John to keep the school going. Students organized evangelistic bands and toured the countryside preaching. Classes were dismissed for lengthy prayer meetings. Students went home to witness to parents. When they returned, they reported miraculous results not only with their parents, but also with people whom they met along the way.

Despite bandits roaming the land and the increasing threat of a Chinese-Japanese war, ordinary Christians became itinerant evangelists visiting every village and feeling perfectly safe.

Services were held anywhere. "Hallelujah! Praise the Lord!" were the greetings. With great joy groups of people gathered together to sing, "O clap your hands, all ye people; shout unto God with the voice of triumph."

Missionaries gathered in various homes, often John and Jewell's, and talked about God's blessings being poured out upon them. They interpreted the experience as an answer to prayer for God to heal the deadness and spiritual famine of the land as well as the chaos and privations that so many were suffering. They felt that the deep hunger created in their midst and the prayer that had gone up as a result was the key.

One of the group introduced a more somber note. "Remember, God always pours out his blessings on his people to prepare them for trial."

In the quiet of their bedroom John and Jewell talked about this after retiring.

"Whatever comes, God has prepared us to face it with joy," John said. "We know now his promises are sufficient for anything."

The revival continued to flourish despite growing tension.

In 1931, as Chiang Kai-shek and his central government fought the rapidly developing Communist Party led by an obscure peasant named Mao Tse-tung, the Japanese occupied Manchuria.

In January of 1932 they bombed Shanghai and then landed soldiers to rape and pillage before withdrawing after a few hours. Still Chiang Kai-shek was convinced his first duty was to fight the Communists. If he let the Japanese have enough rope, he thought, they would hang themselves with foreign intervention.

In striking counterpoint to the blessings being poured out among the Christians in Shantung, China's personal travail deepened in 1934. China was a place where half the populace died before they were thirty years of age. Seventy-five percent of the deaths were due to preventable diseases. The common man suffered from as many as forty-four different kind of taxes. Flood and famine seemed to be the controlling elements of life.

4
Rising Sun

On June 7, 1934, John and Jewell set sail for the United States on an Italian liner, the SS *Conte de Savoia.* It was their second furlough. Their fellow missionaries and Chinese colleagues gave them a grand send-off when they boarded the train in Tsinan for Shanghai. As the train rumbled across the North China countryside, they sat back, clasped hands, and looked at each other contentedly. It had been a rewarding term of service. The excitement of their new walk in the Spirit bubbled within them.

They were starting their tenth year of marriage. There were no children. Jewell had mixed feelings about it. John didn't comment. They knew that at the time many a missionary mother of the North China Mission had lived not long enough to raise her own children in China. They also knew that without children Jewell was as active a missionary as anyone on the field. She was a person with strong opinions, many gifts, much zest, and energy.

Jewell's work with Chinese women had prospered, and John's churches were vibrant with life. Since their experience with the Holy Spirit, their life had grown so full that it seemed to be overflowing all the time.

After they boarded the steamship in Shanghai for their trip to the States, they realized just how hard they had worked. The ship cruised down the coast of China, across the China Sea to Singapore, and then across the Indian Ocean and up through the Suez Canal. Their bodies and minds were recharged in the warm sun that filled the leisure days.

The reality that all the world was not so peaceful struck them sharply when they got to Rome. Their boat was confiscated to transport Italian troops to Abyssinia. There was no doubt about where John and Jewell's sentiments lay: They were with the old Lion of Abyssinia, the emperor Haile Selassie. Italian troops, unopposed despite the emperor's impassioned requests for aid before the League of Nations, were overrunning the ancient land.

John knew that in a matter of time the Japanese could be doing the same thing in Shantung. "This madness may spread," he told Jewell as they sensed Italian war fever and noted the growth of Fascism.

Finally they arranged transportation on another ship, and on July 20, 1934, sailed past the Statue of Liberty into New York Harbor. John and Jewell both had a fierce love for their country. Living in another country only sharpened their patriotism.

They stayed in New York only briefly before boarding the train for Statesville, North Carolina, where they spent a few days with members of John's family.

Early in August they attended the Foreign Mission Conference at Ridgecrest Baptist Assembly in western North Carolina and conferred with their Board's new executive secretary, Charles E. Maddry. Elected in 1932 when the Board was smothered in debt, Dr. Maddry had the seemingly impossible responsibility of leading the Board back to solvency without ceasing missionary effort around the world. He greeted them warmly. John had been a member of Maddry's church when the latter was pastor at Statesville.

Neither the Abernathys nor Maddry mentioned the exchange of correspondence they had the year before. John first wrote his new executive secretary in late 1932 when he shared with him the excitement of the Shantung revival.

"I praise the Lord that he has allowed me to see more people saved and filled with his Spirit than any year before," John wrote. "It's been so in each station of our North China Mission."

Especially important to John and to missionary administrators was the progress toward self-support of the new churches. John wrote Dr. Maddry, "During the past year on the Tsinan field, our city church has become self-supporting financially. In the country field we were permitted to help with two new church buildings which were erected by the Christians on land which they purchased themselves."

John had added, "One is often reminded of the blessings in churches immediately following Pentecost as he sees the sick being healed in answer to prayer, demons cast out, and other signs and wonders which are accompanying the revival as it sweeps through the country." He concluded with a hope that the new secretary would be able to come to China before long.

Maddry had replied warmly. "We are hoping and praying that the fire may catch in America and we may have a great revival in all of our churches in the Southern Baptist Convention."

Less than a year later, however, Maddry's mood changed. Two men, one a missionary in Shantung, journeyed to Richmond and reported to the Foreign Mission Board that in their judgment the revival going on in Shantung was anti-Baptistic and given to excesses of all sorts. They said, "It's more nearly Pentecostalism than anything else."

John Abernathy was named as one of those involved.

Many ministers in Southern Baptist life had received letters of the revival in China. Some wrote Maddry expressing concern and warning that Baptist money would certainly not be forthcoming for such questionable ventures.

Maddry, smarting under his already overwhelming task of leading the Board from debt, wrote a strong letter to John and many of his fellow North China missionaries in the fall of 1933. After citing the charges that had been brought, Maddry wrote, "Please answer at once and give me your views on these matters."

John had replied almost immediately but not before he spent hours in soul-searching. After receiving the letter he had gone to the darkened confines of the Tsinan church to pray, "Lord, give me a good spirit. Lord, help me to be submissive to my brother and patient with these inquiries."

John had known Satan would counterattack. Ample evidence of that could already be seen in Shantung.

Imposters, false prophets, and exploiters, appeared, trying to lead new Christians astray. Yet, God's work proceeded with more power than ever. The more Satan manifested himself, the more strength John and Jewell, their fellow missionaries, and their Chinese colleagues seemed to find in their new walk with Christ through his Spirit.

What cut the Abernathys most deeply in the letter from Maddry was not the terseness of his request, but the realization that one of the men who went to Richmond and presented the charges against them was none other than T. L. Blalock who, representing the China Direct Mission, had recruited John at Southwestern Seminary and Jewell while she was in school in Oklahoma. It was Blalock who shepherded them across the continent in 1920 and led the group that boarded the USS *China Mail*. It was Blalock who helped settle them in Tainan and performed their wedding ceremony. He was a friend, a man who had been a guest in their home and had his feet under their table more times than they could count. That hurt.

Blalock accused the missionaries in Shantung of departing from the historic traditions of the Baptist faith, of practicing Pentecostalism, of embracing the false doctrines of Aimee Semple McPherson, of espousing exotic and dangerous practices.

John and Jewell knew where to take such hurts. In the quiet places where they met the Lord, they found a peace and a poise which sustained them. In this spirit John had answered Dr. Maddry in November of 1933. He responded to each charge and tried to deal with every implication.

He denied inviting Pentecostal missionaries to speak in Baptist churches, though admitted housing such a minister during a time the man's wife was hospitalized in Tsinan. And John had added, "We take no more stock in Mrs. McPherson's strange doctrine than do any others of our Southern Baptist Convention."

He had continued with candor, "Neither my wife nor I have ever spoken in tongues, and I am quite certain there is not a single missionary in our whole North China Mission who would leave the Bible so far as to say speaking in tongues is the only evidence of being filled with the Holy Spirit. We acknowledge with Paul in Corinthians that it is a gift of the Spirit, but not the greatest."

Patiently John had written: "This is more like an old-fashioned revival back home than anything else. I was converted in a meeting in the foothills of North Carolina just like we have been having in our Mission these past three years. Just an old-fashioned Holy Ghost revival. People got happy, and some shouted, 'Hallelujah.' Others groaned under the burden of sin. That's just what we have been and still are seeing here in North China. "Not once have I seen or heard of a missionary jumping or dancing, as Mr. Blalock reports in his letters. Whenever we see Christians appearing to give place to the flesh, we do not hesitate to warn them of the danger."

Of their experience with the Holy Spirit, John wrote, "This was not just ordinary prayer, but carried with it deep heart-searchings to find out what the trouble was and for cleansing. When the cleansing came, the fullness of the Spirit came soon afterwards. It was the same fullness that Moody, Finney, Torrey, the Wesleys, and an innumerable company of others have had. (Acts 1:8: 'But ye shall receive power, after that the Holy Ghost is come upon you: and ye shall be witnesses unto me both in Jerusalem, and in all Judaea, and in Samaria, and unto the uttermost part of the earth.') My wife received this blessing about two weeks before I did, but neither of us 'became blank' or oblivious to what was going on around us as Mr. Blalock charged."

With great feeling John had written, "As to our leaving Baptist faith and principles and going into Pentecostalism, holy-rollerism, etc., I am glad I can say I was never a stronger Baptist in the real sense of the word than I am now." Finally, he wrote, "If letters sent home reporting the revival have caused people to become indifferent to the cause of foreign missions, we're extremely sorry. These reports came from hearts bubbling over with the joy of the Lord and were meant to glorify our blessed Lord and Master, creating a deep hunger in the hearts of our people for a revival, and to stimulate interest in foreign missions."

John concluded, "We are always ready to answer any inquiries that may be made regarding our work here. Everything is open and above board."

Maddry and his associates had been impressed when they read the letter and thanked him not only for his "fine statement," but also for his "Christlike attitude manifested in the whole matter."

But now at Ridgecrest a year later, John wondered if the subject would come up again. It didn't. He even felt free to share his experience and to tell what was happening in Shantung. People were interested, and at night after the meetings, John and Jewell shared with those who came to hear more not only their own experiences, but some of the incredible events they had either seen or heard reported in the midst of the revival.

After the Ridgecrest conference, the Abernathys decided to spend some time at Mr. Leonard's house in Huntington, Arkansas.

A week on the farm was refreshing. Through reading and from porch conversations with the Leonards and neighbors, they were introduced to the American scene including such Roosevelt realities as WPA, NRA, and "New Deal."

In September they moved to Fort Smith, Arkansas, and rented a small apartment for the year. John promised to visit two associations in Louisiana in October, speak at First Baptist Church, Shreveport, and then go to Ardmore, Oklahoma, the latter part of the month.

No sooner had they settled in Arkansas than John received another stern letter from Maddry. The Board's secretary said word had come to the Board that John had accepted an assignment with one of the independent, fundamentalist churches in Ardmore.

John was familiar with the controversy that had flourished during his years in China. Many churches that formerly cooperated with the Southern Baptist Convention had become independent churches or had aligned themselves with small fundamentalist groups. One such church had invited John to speak and he had accepted the invitation, not knowing that it was a noncooperating church until Maddry's letter came.

Maddry wrote, "Have nothing to do with this antimission group in Oklahoma and the Southwest." He revealed his own frustration at having to write such a letter: "I hate to make this request of one of our missionaries because I want to leave them free to speak and act as they wish while in the homeland. But in view of the fact that this group has been fighting our mission work with every unfair means at hand, I am constrained to request that you have nothing to do with them."

John complied. He knew the Board was having a difficult time freeing itself from debt while holding its support in line against charges made by some of the independent groups. But more, John believed it was right to be submissive, insofar as his conscience would allow, to those who exercised a spiritual authority over him.

He laughed at the way the Spirit had tamed his naturally independent spirit. Peace was still there.

But he had little time to worry about it. He and Jewell held Schools of Missions in Arkansas, spoke to the state Woman's Missionary Union meeting in Tulsa, Oklahoma, and then returned to be at key churches in Arkansas for other schools of missions. In November, John spoke in Texas and then went to North Carolina to preach in different churches until mid-December.

Maddry again responded warmly to the spirit John demonstrated. He wrote John asking him to represent the Board at the Illinois state Baptist convention, and also advised him to exercise some moderation in his travels. "Don't wear yourself out," he wrote.

Christmas, a mixture of nostalgia and fellowship, offered the rest and enjoyment John and Jewell needed. Wherever they went they were asked to share their experiences. Friends and new acquaintances quizzed them incessantly about China and the events taking place there.

Newspapers carried stories of Japanese militancy, Chiang Kai-shek's efforts against the Communists, and warnings of all-out war in the Pacific. But increasingly these events were overshadowed by what was transpiring in Europe: the Abyssianian-Italian War and Hitler's power grab in Germany.

Throughout furlough the Abernathys kept in touch with missionaries in Shantung. Mary Crawford wrote faithfully. John was especially concerned over one letter. A missionary couple who had not been caught up in the revival—who, in fact had resisted it—suggested that the school in Tsinan be closed.

John would have agreed with them a few years earlier, feeling that their task should be evangelism and that education was a waste of money. Now he defended the school. He wrote Dr. Maddry at once, stating the role of schools in evangelism. They were necessary to provide leadership for the new churches coming into being. John added that the man who made the suggestion was not Baptistic in doctrine or spirit.

Maddry answered immediately, but the substance of his letter ushered in a sober New Year for John and Jewell.

First, Maddry reassured them about the Tsinan school, indicating that the couple who made the suggestion would probably not be going back to China, then he dealt them a new blow with news that statements and letters had come to the Board from Oklahoma and Texas charging the Abernathys with tendencies toward Pentecostalism.

Maddry pointed out that the charges had been confirmed by staff members who had visited in the area. M. Theron Rankin, the new area secretary for the Orient, felt that the question must be resolved.

"Some understanding should be had with you and Mrs. Abernathy before you return to China," Dr. Maddry wrote. "Therefore, we are going to ask you both to come to Richmond and appear before the Board."

The letter distressed them. Questions John thought he had put to rest in 1933 were there all over again. He spent long hours in prayer, asking God to prepare his heart and his response. Reviewing his experience in Oklahoma and Texas, he felt that it had been positive. People had flocked around him wanting to know more about his walk in the Spirit. Many said they were especially blessed by his messages. Others had responded by volunteering to go to China to preach the gospel. Many made professions of faith.

He did remember one pastor who cautioned him about some of the terms he used. John took the man's advice and revised his approach. He knew there was no way some experiences in the Shantung revival could be communicated without misunderstanding. Yet, once more he was charged with being a Pentecostal, a Holiness, and an independent-minded Baptist.

John's response to Dr. Maddry took three typewritten pages, single spaced. He answered each charge in detail. The spirit of his letter was humble and submissive. He hoped he would not add to the burden carried by Dr. Maddry and Dr. Rankin. "I am a New Testament Baptist and have been nothing else," he reassured them. "If I ever felt I was anything but a Baptist, I would certainly be honest enough to get out of the Baptist church, resign from our Baptist Foreign Mission Board, and go into whatever church I belonged."

He admitted his perplexity over the charges: "We have had the most wonderful response, both in renewed interest in foreign missions and in the need for revival here and around the world."

He ended by saying he would be glad to come to Richmond any time and make a full statement of his experience and his views.

Dr. Maddry answered within days. The Administrative Committee had read John's letter and felt it would not be necessary for him to come to Richmond. Instead, a Board member and a staff member would visit John and Jewell in Little Rock in the spring.

John responded enthusiastically. He and Jewell would be glad to have them.

Meanwhile, the Abernathys continued speaking. Sometimes John went by himself, but Jewell usually went, too. They were increasingly known as a team.

When spring came, the Board's representatives made their visit and talked at length with John and Jewell. They were totally satisfied. Maddry and Rankin both wrote warm letters of reassurance after receiving the report, and the Abernathys began their preparations to return to China.

Over a six-day period in Illinois during the spring, John spoke thirty-one times. The invitations came in response to his presentation at the state convention the previous fall. Reports from such efforts undoubtedly reassured Maddry and Rankin.

John shared only with Jewell his conviction that far more damage would occur from modern or liberal inroads into the work than from the so-called excesses from revival.

"God can defend himself," Jewell reminded John. "We just need to be faithful to him."

Before they sailed for China another problem developed. Slumping contributions for foreign missions caused the Board to cancel all reservations for missionaries scheduled to return to the field in August.

Hastily, John wrote to remind Maddry that he had purchased a round-trip boat ticket in China to save a third of the fare. All he would need to return to China was railroad fare to San Francisco and from Shanghai to Tsinan. "With things as uncertain as they are, we must get back," John wrote.

Just after a hot July 4 in Fort Smith, Maddry telegraphed that they were cleared to go back. Final purchases were made, the packing completed, and their goods shipped to San Francisco.

The trip back was uneventful, though a welcome relief from the hectic schedule they had followed during their twelve-month furlough. Their only uneasiness came from the constant rumors aboard ship that all-out war between Japan and China was inevitable.

Their return to Tsinan was quite a contrast to the last time John and Jewell had returned from furlough. Then the deadness in the churches had been overwhelming. This time renewal of the churches was in evidence. For the first few weeks, friends brought them up to date on the continuing blessings the Lord had wrought. The anxieties and fears of war seemed unimportant in such hours. In turn, their missionary colleagues wanted to know about the United States.

So much was happening in the world that it was hard to keep up. What little information the missionaries got was usually late. They were aware that Pan American had inaugurated a trans-Pacific flying service. Some talked of going home that way on their next furlough. One had read an article which said a German had developed a unique electronic instrument that would send visual images. He called it television.

A woman had flown an airplane from England to South Africa, Margaret Mitchell had written *Gone With the Wind,* and Max Schmelling had defeated Joe Louis for the world's heavyweight championship.

Many of the missionaries had kept up with the Olympics in Berlin in the summer of 1936 and rejoiced over the heroics of an American Negro named Jesse Owen. They all felt the slight when Hitler refused to honor Owen as he honored the white athletes.

They were less aware that Kipling and Houdini had died and that Charlie Chaplin was starring in a movie entitled *Modern Times.*

Of more interest to them were the continuing impact of the depression, the country's efforts to recover, the people's awareness of China's troubles, the price of eggs, and fashions.

Roosevelt was campaigning for a second term when John and Jewell left the States. Two months after they returned to Tsinan, he was easily reelected. Edward the VIII abdicated as king of England to marry an American divorcee, and Italy, after completing her annexation of Abyssinia, struck an alliance with Nazi Germany.

The most bizarre news in 1936 as far as the Abernathys were concerned, however, was the kidnapping of Chiang Kai-Shek by one of his own commanders. The commander was related to the Communist groups with whom Chiang had dealt ruthlessly, and his death was expected at any time.

To John and Jewell's relief it did not come. Instead, an alliance against the Japanese was negotiated and Chiang was released. This gave the Reds breathing room, but it triggered a decision by Japan's military to move into China before the opposition became stronger.

Of course, the missionaries were unaware of this and they breathed a prayer of gratitude when the generalissimo was freed. They turned their faces once again to their work.

Shortly after their return to China, John received a bonus. On a trip to the countryside he encountered the man for whom, in a Buddhist temple some years before, he had prayed for the recovery of a sick son. To John's joy, not only had the man's son recovered but he had also become a Christian and was doing itinerant preaching.

Early in 1937 John took a long preaching trip through western Shantung with W. B. Glass. Dr. Glass, a native of Texas, was one of the veteran missionaries in China. John respected him greatly.

When Charles Maddry had visited Shantung to investigate personally the charges of Pentecostalism in relationship to the revival, it was Dr. Glass' quiet testimony that put Maddry's mind at ease.

Glass had said: "Power in this land has come like the rains that end a great drought. When it begins to rain, the water flows across the country and into the Yellow River, but the river's channel cannot contain it. There is too much of it. The water overflows the channel, spreads across the fields, and knocks down fences and barns. It does some damage, but the drought is broken and the land turns green. That's what happened here spiritually. Our land is green."

When John made his field report in 1937, more than 130 people were awaiting baptism in the churches around Tsinan. There seemed no limit to what the revived churches and missionaries could accomplish. And then a small incident near Peiping changed everything.

At a bridge called Marco Polo a Japanese-provoked exchange of fire became the excuse for an all-out attack by Japanese armies in northern China. They quickly took Peiping and moved on to Shanghai.

John and Jewell were wakened early one morning a few weeks later while vacationing in Tai Shan Mountain. A messenger from the American consul in Tsinan said: "President Roosevelt has ordered all American civilians to leave. You are supposed to gather what you need and move to Tsingtao."

Before the messenger left, John asked him a few questions and then briefed Jewell, who was preparing breakfast.

"What shall we do, John?" she asked.

"Well, I want to do what our President says," replied John, "but I'm not sure that we should leave these people. I don't want you in any danger."

"I'm not in any danger so long as I'm where the Lord wants me," she said. Her voice had the firm assurance John had grown to love and respect.

But the ruthlessness of the Japanese advance convinced him that he should obey the order. They packed after sending a message to

Tsinan to make arrangements with their Chinese brethren to carry on their responsibilities. Then they proceeded to Tsingtao.

There, they were briefed on the Japanese advance, which was moving down the coast toward Shanghai. The world was watching, they were told. They read fairly fresh newspapers for a change and listened to radio broadcasts while they awaited further word. Tremendous sympathy was developing in America for the embattled Chinese and for their leader, Chiang Kai-shek.

The quarters in Tsingtao were crowded, but John and Jewell enjoyed the fellowship. Without children, a reality they now faced as permanent and accepted as God's will to enable both of them to work more effectively, they did not have the same anxieties as did the missionaries with children.

There were 180 Southern Baptist missionaries in China at this time. A good portion of those in North China were in Tsingtao with the Abernathys. Of course, there were Americans on military, government, and commercial assignments among the Tsingtao group, also.

Two weeks later John and Jewell were listening with others to the radio one evening when they heard that Tsinan had been bombed.

"Oh, John," Jewell exclaimed, "our friends!"

The report convinced John that they should return. Despite the urgent pleas of the American consul and of friends, they boarded a train crowded with refugees and made their way back to Tsinan. No sooner had John and Jewell settled into bed the night of their return than they experienced their first bombing attack. The bombs fell far from them, but the noise confirmed the reality of the situation.

The next day John wrote Dr. Maddry: "The battle lines are only thirty miles to the north of us. Enemy planes fly over Tsinan almost daily. . . . Many people have been killed or wounded.

"We have a system of signals to warn of the approach of enemy planes. The first sirens are sounded when planes have been sighted ten miles away, and then when they draw near another signal is given and all the people who have bomb-proof cellers are supposed to take to them and stay until the all-clear signal is sounded."

John tried to express how he and Jewell felt: "Needless to say, we are happy. And in spite of danger, there is a deep and abiding peace in our hearts because we are in the place of God's own divine appointment. When we dedicated our lives to him for service in China, it was strictly unconditional. We had no promise or assurance that we would not be called on by him to serve in places of danger or even to lay down our lives for him if need be."

Many of the Christians in Tsinan felt that the troubles of the day heralded the imminent return of the Lord. Just a few days before, they experienced a terrifying earthquake that caused chimneys to fall, roofs to slide off, walls to cave in, and people to panic. A number of suicides were reported in the city.

One excited citizen reported that "the earth opened and hot lava issued forth."

Jewell found an unusual ministry during this period. She counseled people of means who were unsure what to do. Many of them, trying to preserve their wealth, packed to seek safety elsewhere. She urged them to stay and help. The city was swollen by refugees, and workers were needed to pass out food and clothes. Everywhere were women and children who were hungry, confused, and often in need of medical attention. Jewell and the other women set up centers in the churches to help.

The Christians adopted a watchword: "But when ye shall hear of wars and rumors of wars, be ye not terrified."

In November word came that Shanghai had fallen after a terrible loss of life.

John wrote Maddry that the Chinese government had decided to sell out Shantung. Disappointed with Chiang Kai-Shek's move, he nevertheless urged prayer for the general and his wife.

Shortly after December 12, John and Jewell heard of the horrible events that transpired when the Japanese took Nanking. "The Rape of Nanking" with the death of thousands of civilians, wholesale ravishing and pillage, shocked the whole world. Yet no one came to China's aid, as Chiang Kai-shek thought they would. The Japanese pressed on.

By Christmas Day in 1937 the city of Tsinan was under continual bombardment. There were no Christmas parties. Refugees by the thousands trudged by the compound, fleeing from the Japanese. By nightfall the roads were crowded with retreating Chinese soldiers.

The day after Christmas John and Jewell were awakened by explosions. They gathered their belonging to take cover before they realized that no planes were in the air. John decided the noise was artillery fire and ran outside to question the soldiers running through the streets. He learned that the explosions were set off by the Chinese army. They were blowing up buildings and utilities before leaving.

"The explosions were like earthquakes, and smoke from burning buildings reminded me of the description of Sodom and Gomorrah," John noted.

John was shocked at what war did to people. Buildings and warehouses were looted. He watched frightened people snatch things that were of no value or use to them. How grateful he was for the way Christians responded! Prayer was constant. There was joy in the midst of anxiety.

John and Jewell slept very little that night. The next morning they stood at the door as Japanese army contingents came down the road. They noticed the quietness of the people and were struck with the confidence of the Japanese troops. While the retreating Chinese soldiers had been ill fed and ill equipped, the Japanese men appeared to be well fed and well equipped.

Though John had no respect for the Japanese cause and was incensed at their ruthlessness, he had to admit they seemed to know what they were doing in Tsinan. They quickly brought order out of chaos. Transportation resumed, food arrived, government offices that had been all but paralyzed by corruption and confusion operated smoothly.

The following day John met with Japanese authorities. He was assured that as American citizens he and his wife would be completely protected and that his work would continue. There were a few regulations with which to deal and, of course, John was cautioned that his work in the country must be cut back because of guerrilla activity there.

"We cannot insure your protection there, Mr. Abernathy," the Japanese official said benignly.

As John walked back to the house to share his findings with Jewell, he realized they were no longer in free China.

5

Gripsholm

Jewell Abernathy's hand rested lightly on her husband's shoulder, but her usually smiling face grimaced at the shrill sounds from the radio he was trying to tune.

"The only time I have trouble with this thing is when I'm trying to get the news," John said with exasperation.

"Shhhh!" Jewell said. "That's it!"

Quietly they listened, and then caught their breath as the newscaster reported that severe damage had been inflicted on Tsining when Chinese forces there had tried to make a stand. The Japanese aerial bombing had dislodged the Chinese defenders. John and Jewell took an even sharper breath when the newscaster reported that a missionary compound occupied by Americans had been heavily damaged and some lives lost.

"Oh, John! Bertha!" Jewell was on the verge of tears.

"I'll try to get over there tomorrow morning and check," John decided. "But I feel sure she's okay. They would have mentioned any American injuries specifically."

Bertha Smith was the only Southern Baptist missionary in Tsining. She had insisted on staying there, whatever came. Strong in prayer, her faith in matters large and small had always encouraged John and Jewell. They had enjoyed Christian fellowship with her since the early days of the Shantung Revival.

Early the next morning John went to Japanese military headquarters to get a permit to travel to Tsining.

"Oh, it is much too dangerous," the Japanese major who dealt with him said. "We could not allow you to take your car to Tsining."

But to John's surprise, the officer volunteered a military escort to drive him to Tsining to check on Bertha. The major had heard that the mission compound was damaged, and he wanted to apologize on behalf of the Japanese government.

After an anxious trip to Tsining, John's relief was immense when he found Bertha Smith calm and poised. She was comforting refugees and helping care for the wounded. Among the dead in the city was one who worked in the Baptist compound.

Bertha was nearly ill, however, from lack of sleep. John urged her to return with him to Tsinan. He was not surprised when she refused.

John and the Japanese major investigated the damage and estimated the cost of repairs. To John's delight, the major insisted on giving $6,500 to the Mission to aid in repairs. He pointed out that it was not indemnity money, but an expression of sympathy and goodwill.

Life in Tsinan took on a new urgency and a new excitement for John and Jewell. Jewell confessed, "There comes a hesitancy every time I pray for peace to come to China when I see rich and poor turning to him as never before."

In a letter—carefully worded because of Japanese censorship—she reported that she was teaching the book of Kings at the woman's Bible school. The reference was a hidden call to prayer, since the passages spoke of deliverance from oppressors.

She also requested prayer for one of the Chinese evangelists who was being held by robbers for $3,000 ransom. Even war could not change some things.

Despite limitations imposed by the Japanese and by danger from bandits, John baptized ninety-nine converts in the summer.

Moving about in the countryside became increasingly difficult. One night they had to turn back from the Tawen River because of a destroyed bridge. As they were returning home, their car slipped from the road and became hopelessly mired. Just before dark several coolies came along, and John persuaded them to help him dislodge the car, but as darkness fell they knew they would never make it back to Tsinan. They stopped at a little village to spend the night.

The Abernathys had visited the village before, but now they hardly recognized it. Doors, windows, and furniture were gone from every house. They had been burned to keep the people warm. It was obvious there was no place for visitors to stay, so John rented two quilts for thirty cents and they huddled in the back of the car to await dawn.

"Are you warm?" John asked. Jewell was perennially healthy, but he was always solicitous of her welfare.

"Like a bug in a rug," she replied. "John?"

"Yes."

"I don't hear any dogs."

I know. You don't hear dogs when people are hungry."

John shifted his weight to look out the back window, then to each side.

"Do you think we'll be safe?" she asked softly.

"We'll be okay." He moved close to her again. "God has a battalion of angels around us right now!"

"How do you know?"

"How do you know he doesn't?"

They made their way home the next day, bringing great relief to their Chinese colleagues who had feared they might be in the hands of bandits.

Jewell's work was greatly strengthened by the addition of a new worker to the Tsinan field, a young woman named Jenny Alderman Jenny, as fair and petite as Jewell was dark and full bodied, went with her into the villages to hold Bible schools for women.

At one village they noticed a group of Christians who, they knew had been walking since well before daylight to get to the school One of the women, wife of a newly ordained pastor with whose family John and Jewell had spent some time, carried a four-year-old she called Baby-Truth. The child demanded that his mother put him down

"Why?" the mother asked.

"Because," said the child, "I want to bow to Shepherd Mother Abernathy."

Laughing heartily, Jewell bowed in return, then picked the child up and and gave him a big bear hug.

After school Jewell and Jenny visited homes. In some they watched the women work with spinning wheels and clumsy looms, twisting hemp for rope. As they walked about dodging pigs that ran between their feet, the two women stopped to speak to any who seemed open to discussion.

Twice they were asked to give counsel. One woman's conscience was deeply moved when she attended the services. She was obviously in distress. The year before she had starved her baby girl to death and she wanted to know if such a sin could be forgiven. Patiently the two women explained to her the gospel of forgiveness in Jesus Christ.

Another woman was listening. She in turn confessed that she had put her baby girl out to freeze on a snowy night years before. As tears rolled down her eyes, she said, "I am still haunted by her cries."

Jewell tried to help Jenny become accustomed to being stared at. One of the Chinese women did not face the speaker during a whole service, but turned around to stare at the two Americans. This woman, one of the older Chinese women, later told the blue-eyed Jenny, "When you have been here as long as Mrs. Abernathy and quit drinking milk and eat more of our food, you too will look like us."

"But," Jenny explained, "Mrs. Abernathy has always been dark and has had black hair since infancy."

"Oh, no!" said the Chinese woman. "We remember when she came. She was very fair, just like you."

Jewell believed the woman spoke the truth as she saw it. The people did not see the difference in her they once did. "Praise the Lord!"

Travel into the country became more and more difficult through 1939 and 1940. Bandits, thugs, and guerrilla bands resisting the Japanese made the countryside all but uninhabitable. People began to suffer from lack of food and were unable to carry on their normal life-style. A heavy drought in 1939 reduced the harvest and made the ground almost too dry to plant again.

John and Jewell invited one of the new missionary families from the language school at Peiping, the Baker James Cauthens, to spend Christmas with them in 1939. The Cauthens and their two young children had arrived in China only a few months before. Cauthen had been serving as missions professor at Southwestern Seminary in Fort Worth when John and Jewell spoke there during their last furlough. When John heard that Baker and Eloise were being appointed, he remarked to Jewell, "I'm not surprised. When we visited them in Fort Worth, I thought he asked a lot of pointed questions."

A daughter of W. B. Glass, Eloise had grown up in North China. The Abernathys had known her as a schoolgirl. They were impressed with a family who would volunteer to come to China during such difficult days.

John and Jewell had expected it to be only a short time before the war would be over and China again united. Now, with the Japanese entrenched up and down the coast and the borders of Free China pushed back deeply into the interior, they were not sure. News from Europe was equally discouraging. Hitler had invaded Poland, and Britain and France had declared war on Germany. John and Jewell knew the difficulties ahead would be formidable. They prayed for strength.

One night an unusual sound awakened John from a deep sleep. His heart seemed to jump into his throat as he became aware that several men were standing around his bed. He raised up to be caught by beams of light from several flashlights. In their glare he could see hands holding revolvers. Jewell woke with a start.

"Stay calm," John told her. "Stay calm."

"What do you want?" he asked the men, trying to keep his voice even.

One of the men behind the circle of light replied. "We shall answer you after we see what you have."

"You are glad to share your wealth, aren't you?" another said.

"We have no wealth," John replied.

"Enough," the obvious leader said sternly. "Come, show us your house. We will decide for ourselves how wealthy you are."

In the next moments, John moved and spoke carefully. He knew these men could be ruthless. People had died at the hands of such groups.

"Missionary! If this is all you have, you are not following a very rich God. You should change Gods."

Shortly before dawn the men left, having done John and Jewell no personal harm, but relieving them of some of "this world's goods."

Strangely, the Abernathys found the incident encouraging. It helped them realize that things are not important. God's presence had been real. They felt stronger than ever and were able to identify with Chinese brothers who had often been robbed and ill treated.

Despite Japanese occupation, John hoped in 1940 to complete a new church building in the center of Tsinan. Most of the funds had been given at great sacrifice by people who were suffering much. "How can such a thing be done in the midst of such hardships?" John and Jewell often asked each other, giving themselves to grateful prayer.

Dedication of the church building brought missionaries from all over Shantung Province and became the occasion for revival. At Mission meeting in Tsingtao a few days later, John reported between seven and eight hundred additions to the churches in the Tsinan field during the 1939-40 period.

Meanwhile, tension began to build from increased problems between Japan and the United States. There was talk about war being inevitable between the United States and Japan. The North China Mission agreed late in 1940 that any missionary should feel free to return immediately to the United States. Each family was asked to make its own decision on the matter.

Early in 1941 three American ships arrived to evacuate American personnel from China. New pressures were placed on the missionaries to leave. Some argued that all wives and children should be evacuated.

Jewell took a dim view of the idea and told John the United States government did not bring her to China, the Foreign Mission Board did not bring her to China, John didn't even bring her to China, but God brought her to China. She wrote a friend about her perplexity: "The question is shall we be loyal to the government and obey its instructions at this time, or have we higher orders that we must obey?"

As the only Southern Baptist missionaries in the Tsinan station, John, Jewell, and Mary Crawford met together to pray about the matter. A third urgent letter had come from the State Department asking all American citizens to evacuate. They agreed to pray quietly and individually and then share their impressions. John had full assurance that Jewell should go. Jewell wasn't sure.

Throughout that night she sought God's will.

God spoke to her through Exodus 33:14, "My presence shall go with thee, and I will give thee rest." She felt that the passage contained her marching orders. The next day she tearfully began to pack.

Jewell thought her heart would break when she sailed from Shanghai on April 20, leaving John. They had been separated briefly before, many times in fact. But now they had no knowledge of when they might be reunited.

Unable to board ship when they arrived in Shanghai, John and Jewell registered at a hotel to await the sailing of her boat. As she unpacked her things, she noticed a passage of Scripture tacked to the wall over the old-fashioned dresser. She moved closer to read it.

"Thank you, Lord," she said. The Scripture was once more Exodus 33:14, "My presence shall go with thee. . . ."

She needed the added assurance more than she realized.

Jewell felt pangs of guilt on ship. The food was excellent, her cabin luxurious. But the contrast of their recent years in Tsinan was too radical. She kept thinking about John.

When the ship put into Pearl Harbor for a brief stop, Jewell renewed friendships with the Charles Leonards—no relation, but friends who had previously served in China.

"Why don't you and John work here until the war is over?" they asked.

That sounded good to Jewell. She wrote John immediately, saying that if he felt he had to leave China they might consider working in Honolulu. In the same letter, however, she said she was hoping she could be back by his side before Christmas.

Upon arrival in San Francisco, she was greeted by a letter of welcome and concern from Dr. Maddry. He urged her to get a physical examination and plan to attend Foreign Mission Week at Ridgecrest.

First, she had to go home to Arkansas to find a place to live. She and John had agreed that, because her father's house was crowded, she should rent a room in Fort Smith where they had stayed on their last furlough. But the lure of family was too strong, and she put her suitcases down in Huntington with her family.

After Ridgecrest and a heavy summer schedule of speaking, she bought an accordion and settled down in Huntington to learn to play it.

"It will be great for women's meetings when I get back to Tsinan," she wrote John.

In Huntington, Jewell was Zenobia once more.

"Aunt Zenobia, why do you always speak Chinese?" a niece asked.

"Because her heart is in China," a nephew answered before their aunt could speak.

Sitting on the porch, practicing her accordion but letting her mind wander, Jewell knew that was true. She heard far too little from John, and what she heard made her anxious.

He had written in July, "I feel the lid is going to blow any time now." At the time, he was in Hwanghsien where he and several other missionaries had gone to arrange transfer of the seminary there to

Chinese in case Americans were driven out. Jewell learned later that John and two Chinese preachers with him had been stopped by Japanese soldiers on the way back to Tsinan and roughed up. A few weeks later while in Tsingtao on Mission business his travel permit was "frozen" and it was two weeks before he could break through red tape to get back to Tsinan. There he found Baptist property "frozen," with two sentries stationed outside. A few days later he discovered that his bank account, too, had been "frozen" by the Japanese.

Jewell's heavy speaking schedule kept her from worrying too much. She was in Illinois for three weeks, and then in Oklahoma and Louisiana. When she returned home to Fort Smith, she found two letters. One from the Foreign Mission Board brought the sad news that P. E. White, one of the missionaries left behind in China, had died. The other letter, from one of John's relatives, indicated worry because Abernathy men tended to die from heart trouble in their forty-seventh year. The next year would be John's forty-seventh.

Jewell took the anxiety provoked by the two letters to the Lord in searching prayer. Once more she found the peace she had learned to expect from the Lord.

She received an encouraging word the next day in a letter from a State Department officer she and John had known in Tsinan. He was hoping to return to China in December, and if he made it, she might be able to return, also. She made application and later in the month received word that she had a tentative sailing date from San Francisco on December 7, 1941.

Jewell read the newspapers avidly, though they played "yo-yo with her emotions." One day she read reports of new peace initiatives in Asia, and the next day of new war threats. When, early in November, she received word that the December 7 sailing date had been cancelled, she cried long into the night.

Letters from John continued to worry her. They had not been able to get funds, he reported, but the Chinese were taking up collections for his support.

"I wonder what you were doing yesterday," he wrote. "I do not know how many times I've dreamed about you. Once I dreamed you suddenly appeared here and I was so pleased and surprised I couldn't speak for a minute; then we both said, 'God surely worked a miracle this time.' It was all so real that I am still thinking about it. God is able to work miracles; in fact, we see him do it almost daily here. I wish he would work one for us and open the way for you to come back."

The Foreign Mission Board wrote Jewell around the first of December that since she could not get back to China, they would authorize John to take a furlough early in 1942. Dr. Maddry urged her to take it easier. He said her report indicated she had been speaking at too many Kiwanis and Rotary Clubs in addition to churches and schools of missions.

On Sunday morning, December 7, Jewell and her family went to church where she spoke twice. Afterwards they joined friends for dinner. While they were eating, neighbors came with the news that Pearl Harbor had been attacked. Japan and the United States were at war.

On the other side of the international date line, John awoke on the morning of December 8 (in America, December 7) and wondered about the day ahead. He thought perhaps he could catch the morning news broadcast. The night before he had listened attentively to news about a German advance on Moscow. Continuing tension was reported between the United States and Japan.

Following his devotions, he dressed and joined his houseboy, whose activities had already filled the house with the appetizing smells of breakfast.

As he walked by his desk, John was tempted to read his last letter from Jewell one more time. Nothing bothered him so much as not hearing from her for long periods. It was obvious that she wasn't getting his letters. and he knew she had written many times since the last one he received.

A sudden loud banging at the front door startled John. His houseboy looked perplexed. John motioned him to stay put while he went to see who was there. As he opened the door, a Japanese officer shoved him aside roughly and swaggered into the house, slapping the side of his trousers with a riding crop. A dozen heavily armed soldiers followed the officer inside.

"What's the meaning of this?" John asked. He did not want to antagonize the obviously nervous group, but he tried to appear firm.

"You have not heard?" the officer asked, surprised.

"Heard what?"

"Our countries are at war, Mr. Abernathy. The American counsul can no longer protect you, so it will be necessary for us to protect you."

"Am I a prisoner?" John asked.

"Well, let us say, you are a special prisoner," the officer answered.

"Does that mean especially good or especially bad?" John's irritation overrode his rising anxiety.

The Japanese officer's face turned hard. "We know you are a special agent for your government and that you have a radio sending set somewhere here."

"I am no agent for anyone except Jesus Christ," John said.

"Oh, come now, Mr. Abernathy! No one would stay in this country this long unless he had a clandestine assignment."

John was pushed aside as a search of the house continued. They marched him upstairs and asked him to show them where he kept his radio sending set.

"I have no radio sending set," John said.

Without warning, the officer slapped him.

John reeled. Everything in him wanted to retaliate. He felt a rising flush as he started to return the blow. Realizing that he would only provoke harm, he recovered his pose and stood silently.

When further search revealed nothing, the contingent departed after telling him that there would be guards at the door. He would not be allowed to leave his house.

"Consider yourself a prisoner," the officer said, slamming the door.

After they left John was overcome with deep remorse. "God forgive me. I have been an unfaithful witness."

Head bowed, he remembered how Jesus was struck, spat upon, and scourged without every replying in anger. He went to his bedroom, fell on his knees, and sought God's forgiveness. "God, give me strength for this trial before me," he added. He also prayed for Jewell. "She must know by now that our country is at war," he said half aloud. "I'll bet she is beside herself with worry."

Active by nature, John's house arrest was oppressive. He spent the days in study, Bible reading, and prayer. Some relief came with the Chinese Christian workers who were allowed to visit him. They gave him the opportunity to plan and continue his work through them.

At the time John was placed under house arrest, he had no funds available and was unable to secure access to any of the Board's resources for which he was responsible. But Chinese Christians began delivering food to the house and he nearly always had enough to eat.

One afternoon two Japanese soldiers came into the house and called for him. When he came, one of them began to slap his face. John realized that the methodical slapping was designed to promote some kind of retaliation on his part. Praying silently, he offered the other cheek as Scripture enjoined him. His act of acceptance killed whatever anticipation the sadistic soldier nourished, and he and his colleague soon retreated.

Again John retired to his room. This time to thank God for the strength and peace that had been his.

During this time John received no news except what the Japanese told him. According to them, the Hawaiian Islands had been captured and the American navy completely destroyed. He was told that the Japanese had taken all the American bases in the Pacific Islands, including the Philippines, and that they had captured Thailand, Hong Kong, Burma, Singapore, and Indonesia.

Soldiers again came into the house early in March. They told John to prepare an overnight bag. A Japanese colonel arrived soon after and announced that he was taking over John's house.

"You will be moved to a concentration camp with the other American spies," the officer said.

The colonel cautioned John as he packed, "Now, remember, Mr. Abernathy, you are to take nothing more than the things you use every day. Do you understand?"

John nodded. He was not sure what was ahead, but he felt very much at peace. The long days of prayer and Bible study had done their work.

John was interned at Cheloo University. Upon arrival, he found that he was among nearly a hundred American and British missionaries, along with some American diplomatic personnel.

Things were more difficult at Cheloo than during house arrest. While prisoners were seldon abused, food was scarce and disease rampant. Within a short time all were suffering from dysentery. They were

John and Jewell Abernathy on their wedding day, June 20, 1925, in China

John and Jewell "side by side"—symbolic of their devotion to Christ and to each other

The Abernathys pose with their fellow Christians shortly after beginning work in China (circa 1925).

John and Jewell, along with the faculty of True Light Baptist School, Tsinan, Shantung, China (January 3, 1936)

(Left) John Abernathy served as president of the Korean Baptist Seminary, Taejon, Korea. His able vice-president was Rev. Hoh Dam Vice. (Right) Brother Abernathy loved to play the piano for the children at the Inchon Orphanage, Inchon, Korea.

Brother Abernathy with the faculty of the Zion Baptist Academy, Inchon, Korea.

The Abernathys fellowship with Deacon Dyer (left) and Dr. R. G. Lee (second from right) in front of the Seoul Memorial Baptist Church, Seoul, Korea.

The Abernathys help celebrate John's sixtieth birthday Korean-style (1957).

John and Jewell Abernathy at Glorieta (N.M.) Baptist Assembly in the summer of 1960

not isolated, however, and gained much spiritual reinforcement from fellowship.

As John dressed from day to day, he noticed his weight falling rapidly. The time came when he could get three fingers in his collar after he buttoned it, and his belt began to lap his trousers. He soon had to punch extra holes in it.

As he returned from the washroom one morning, a Japanese soldier on watch grabbed his elbow, saying, "What's wrong with your arm?"

Looking down, John noticed that his elbow, which had been troubling him, was swollen. Although the soldier's touch did not hurt, John decided to yelp fervently. The soldier looked concerned and said, "Dress, and come with me."

John followed him through the camp to an office where a German doctor was quartered. The doctor motioned for the soldier to stand outside the office while he examined the patient.

He spoke to John in precise English, "Relax, my friend, I'm not one of Hitler's Germans."

The doctor led John to the examining table and began to look at his arm.

"It doesn't really bother me," John said. "But I felt that complaining about it might lead to an opportunity like this."

"Did you know the Americans had bombed Tokyo?" the doctor asked.

"No," John said. "I've only heard of American defeats."

"A man named Doolittle led them." The doctor manuevered John's arm, "Does that hurt?"

"No. It's a bit sore though."

"Yes, that raid over Tokyo shook up the Japs quite a bit. They didn't get all the American navy at Pearl Harbor, either."

"Thank God," John said softly.

"Let's put this in a sling," the doctor said of John's arm. "It should get better if you don't use it for awhile."

He prepared the sling and then opened the door and instructed the soldier to return John in a few days. Then turning to John he said, "I'll make you a cup of tea."

"God bless you," John said.

His eyes glistened as he followed the prodding of the soldier back to the internment area.

The doctor helped the elbow, but what he did for John's spirits was far more important.

Many of the missionaries at Cheloo had been together in the Shantung revival. In their prayer sessions together, they expressed conviction that God's purpose in the revival was partly to provide additional resources for such a time as this.

They learned to praise God for their circumstances. Somehow, they believed their imprisonment would be used for his glory.

The camp erupted with joy in early June when word came that America and Japan had agreed to repatriate, on a man-for-man basis, the citizens each was holding. Forty-six Americans, including John, were selected from the Tsinan group at Cheloo and put on a special train for Shanghai on June 13. On the train John found that Charles Culpepper was among those chosen from another detention center.

John bade farewell to his Chinese friends. Many of them had visited him regularly, weeping for joy when they found him in good health, wringing their hands with concern at his weight loss and wrapped-up arm. Many times a visitor surreptitiously ripped open the corner of a coat and handed him money with which to buy food. They told him of people being saved in the churches and of the work of Chinese missionaries sent out to witness in the countryside. John told them of his conviction that God was using all the privations and horror to open an effectual door into the hearts of the Chinese.

Though rumor had it they would board a ship almost immediately, the group being repatriated was detained for two weeks in a concentration camp outside Shanghai. When they boarded the SS *Conte Verde* on June 29, they were still prisoners under Japanese control. The soldiers admonished them, "Be sure to tell them we treated you right, and don't pray for the United States."

The *Verde* sailed first to Hong Kong. There she was boarded by another group of Americans to be exchanged. Among many Southern Baptist missionaries boarding at Hong Kong was Orient secretary, Dr. M. Theron Rankin. There was a warm reunion with prayers and praise for their deliverance.

Next the ship set sail for Singapore for still another load of Americans to be repatriated, then sailed across the Indian Ocean for Lorenco Marques, in Portugese South Africa, neutral territory designated as the site for the exchange.

During the voyage, the missionaries pooled their meager information. They still had little real knowledge of the war's progress. It served to remind them they were still Japanese prisoners. Allowed to hold Sunday services, the missionaries were instructed not to sing "God, Bless America."

They reached the harbor of Lorenco Marques in early evening. As the *Verde* dropped anchor, John and his fellow missionaries could see another ship at anchor a few hundred yards away. It was the SS *Gripsholm,* a Swedish ship, loaded with Japanese exchange prisoners from America.

The lights of the *Gripsholm* were bright, glimmering across the waters between the ships. Most of the Americans on the *Conte Verde* were soon at the rail looking longingly at their deliverance. John could stand it no longer. In a strong voice he began to sing, "God bless America, land that I love. . . ." Charles Culpepper, at his side, looked at him in surprise and then joined him. Soon the whole company was singing "God, Bless America." The Japanese made no move to stop them.

The next day a parade of Japanese and Americans—men, women, and children—passed each other transferring between the *Conte Verde* and the *Gripsholm.* There were many good-natured remarks between them, since most of the repatriated Japanese spoke English. The children especially enjoyed the verbal interplay.

Soon John and the other Americans were safely on board the *Gripsholm.* It was almost like being in the homeland. At last they knew they were free! They hugged each other and prayed and sang at will.

The *Gripsholm* was boldly colored and broadly identified because German submarines still roamed the Atlantic. Its passengers gave little thought to that as they filed into the dining halls, where steaming American food waited for them.

By the time the *Gripsholm* docked temporarily in Rio de Janeiro in late July, John had regained some of the fifty pounds he lost during his internment.

Two Southern Baptist missionary families living in Brazil, the Porters and Olivers, were waiting when they landed at Rio. They took the whole group on a tour of the colorful city. John especially enjoyed the trip to Sugar Loaf Mountain. The other missionaries kidded him at his propensity to keep looking north. Late in the day he dispatched a telegram to Jewell, asking her to meet him in New York.

On the voyage north they were more conscious of submarines and mines. The most anxious moment came when they passed the burning hulk of a merchant ship. Twice the *Gripsholm* circled the metal pyre to look for survivors. None were found. A grizzled old seaman told John that in all probability the U-boat had surfaced and machine gunned those who abandoned ship. When the *Gripsholm* finally steamed away from the sinking hulk, a quiet, subdued group stood at the rail, watching until the doomed ship disappeared over the horizon.

Several alerts and "abandon ship" drills followed. It was only as the *Gripsholm* steamed past the familiar lines of the Statue of Liberty in the early dawn of August 25 that John and his fellow passengers really felt sure they were going to make it. The American ambassador, who was the leader of the returnees, was moved deeply at the sight. He stood before the silent, tearful group, and recited a portion of "The Man Without a Country."

> Breathes there a man with soul so dead
> Who never to himself has said,
> "This is my own, my native land."

Jewell Abernathy was alternately excited and frustrated about her schedule. Though requests for speaking engagements were flooding in, and the Board was asking her to go first to Illinois and later to Louisiana, she did not accept any of them. She wanted to be free in September.

"John is coming home," she said. "I just know it."

When Maddry called her with news that John was supposed to be among those repatriated on the *Gripsholm,* she cried with joy. She kept the mails busy with letters to Richmond, asking where she could meet him.

She planned to go to North Carolina to wait for him, but when his telegram came from Rio, she was immediately New York bound. She met the party of well-wishers, including Dr. Maddry, in New York the day before the *Gripsholm* was due.

For Dr. Maddry, it was an especially poignant moment. He had been caught in Honolulu during the bombing of Pearl Harbor. On his return to Richmond he had plunged immediately into efforts to secure the return of the missionaries in Japanese-held territory. Miraculously, there had been only one loss of life. Missionary Rufus Gray had either been killed or had died following a Japanese interrogation in the Philippines. Maddry broke down in tears when he was assured of the repatriation of most of the others.

His leadership of the Foreign Mission Board covered ten of its rockiest years. Now the opportunity to pay off the debt was in sight, and new advance was being planned even during wartime retrenchment. The Southern Baptist Convention met in San Antonio in 1943 and appointed a committee of nineteen for post-war planning, including among other things, a broad missionary expansion. But Dr. Maddry felt that his days of leadership were over, that it was time to release the reins to a younger man. In his mind this younger man was coming home on the *Gripsholm*, his name was M. Theron Rankin.

Early the morning of August 25, Jewell Abernathy and the other missionary wives and relatives awakened in the hotel rooms where they had been registered by the Foreign Mission Board. She dressed and redressed. Everything had to be just right. Finally, her excitement overwhelmed such concerns. She left with the others before daylight for the building from which they could see the ship's arrival. Her heart jumped at the sight. The boldly colored *Gripsholm* was beautiful and somewhere on it was John.

On the *Gripsholm*, John and Charles Culpepper scanned the crowds intently, but saw nobody they knew.

First, the mail came on board. From it the Southern Baptist missionaries learned that their loved ones would meet them at a nearby building and from there go to the hotel where accommodations had been made for all.

All day the missionaries were inspected, interrogated, and debriefed. They had to draw maps and provide information the government thought it could utilize. Toward evening they were released. Maddry met them and led them to the building where the emotionally charged reunion was held.

As John held Jewell in his arms, he whispered, "Let's not ever get separated again."

Voiceless, she nodded and held him tighter.

6
Free China

Before John's return, Jewell told friends that she wanted a second honeymoon. It was indeed that—for a time. They stayed in New York for a week, then visited John's relatives in North Carolina before going to Arkansas to set up housekeeping once more in Fort Smith. Jewell waited on John hand and foot and particularly enjoyed interpreting the changed American scene for him.

Wartime America was far different from the sluggish postdepression scene they witnessed on their furlough in 1935.

Everywhere men in uniform were on their way overseas. Women in slacks were on their way to work in factories. It was the day of Rosie the Riveter, war bonds, paper drives. Betty Grable was America's favorite pinup girl. People flocked to the movies to see the heroics of the English in a Greer Garson film called *Mrs. Miniver.*

News from the war fronts was mixed. The Russians held the Germans at Stalingrad at great cost of life to both sides. But Germany was unleashing on England a new kind of hell called the V-2 rocket.

The United States landed troops at Guadalcanal for an offensive move that brought an end to eight months of retreat. From his base in Australia, Douglas MacArthur reinforced his vow to return to the Philippines.

And John made his vow—to return to China. In church encampments, missions conferences, civic clubs, and schools, he told of China's heroic struggle. He made 252 addresses during the first eight months after his repatriation.

He and Jewell asked for prayer for the Chinese, who were suffering greatly. Shantung was reporting a major famine. They called for relief funds, and commitment for missionary service in order to buy up the opportunity that would surely emerge as soon as the war was over.

John was not alone in his resolve to go back. Jewell insisted that when he returned, she would be by his side. She had enough separation.

Yet separation was the order of the day as they accepted invitations to different parts of the country to speak on missions. Jewell accompanied Woman's Missionary Union secretaries in Louisiana, Oklahoma, and Arkansas on church tours and went to several schools of missions. John did the same thing in Texas, Oklahoma, and Missouri.

They were flattered when John received an invitation from Dr. Rankin to speak during Foreign Missions Week at Ridgecrest. And the chance to renew fellowship with other displaced missionaries and foreign missions' most avid supporters were exciting to both of them.

At night, after the sessions ended, John and Jewell gathered with other China missionaries to discuss possibilities of getting back. Dr. Rankin, who had become executive secretary of the Foreign Mission Board, urged them to be patient and to realize what a tremendous impact they were having on the home churches. But the possibility of continued work in Free China was irresistible to John and Jewell.

In the fall of 1943, John was asked by the Department of Navy to fill out applications for interpreter's service. He did so, though he had no assurance that was what he should do. With so many men in uniform, however, he felt he needed to be available for whatever purpose the government might be able to use him. Nothing came of the applications.

John and Jewell filed applications in early 1944 for visas to go to Free China. In April they were turned down—for the second time. Both were discouraged. The battle lines in China had stabilized, and there was real opportunity for ministry in Chinese-held territory.

Returning from a speaking engagement one day a few hours ahead of Jewell, John found a registered letter from Washington, D.C. Dr. Frank Price, representing the Chinese government, was organizing a group of missionaries to return to China to serve in a Chinese government training program for interpreters. Dr. Price, a prominent Presbyterian missionary, wrote:

"The Chinese government has proposed a limited number of well selected Chinese-speaking Americans be engaged immediately for various forms of liaison work either by the American army or Chinese government or both.

". . . As a result of discussions in Chungking and Washington, the War Department is now ready to engage immediately ten or twelve men as civilian employees to assist in interpretation relations with Chinese-student interpreters. . . . Those who go out in civilian capacities will be engaged by the War Department. . . . Others may be commissioned as officers. . . . The smaller number who might be engaged by the Chinese government would be on a contract with the Chinese government and paid by them.

"Will you kindly let me know as quickly as possible whether you are ready to consider the war service in China proposed in this letter? . . ."

At the close of the letter Dr. Price explained that John's longtime friend, Dr. R. A. Torrey, Jr., had submitted John's name as someone qualified for the project.

John's heart raced as he read the letter and thought of the possibilities it offered. Then he realized that Jewell would not be able to go with him. Being separated with speaking engagements was hard enough. The possibility of another such separation as they had experienced when he remained in China was too much. Yet, they had prayed for an opportunity to return, and this seemed to be an answer—at least for John.

When Jewell came in, he listened to her excited account of her week in Louisiana and then he laid the letter before her. She read it silently and looked up, her eyes big and moist, "God has answered our prayer, hasn't he, John?"

He started to say something, but she went on.

"Not quite the way we asked, of course. But when we lay problems before him, we have to accept his solution, don't we?"

Too choked to speak, John reached for her and held her tightly. Then they knelt and prayed a prayer of thanksgiving.

On the first day of June, 1944, John checked into the Prince George Hotel in New York City to join the group with which he would journey to Free China. A letter from Dr. Rankin awaited him. As the desk clerk handed him the familiar envelope, he quickly opened it—half afraid it was a word that might prevent his going.

"I will not try to express what I feel in my heart about your response to the chance of going back to China," Rankin wrote. "I can comprehend in some measure, the meaning of what you have committed yourself to. I think of the words that Jesus said to Peter: Thou art a rock, and upon this rock I will build my church. Truly God's kingdom has been built through the ages upon the faith and allegiance of such servants in his kingdom as you are."

John winced a bit at the praise. He was doing what he wanted to do; it did not take heroics. His only difficulty was having to leave Jewell.

Rankin's letter went on to assure John of the Board's provision for Jewell during the time he would be overseas.

Folding the letter, he went to his room, unpacked, secured a sheet of hotel stationery from the writing desk, and penned a note to Dr. Rankin. He thanked him for his letter and for his encouragement "Above all," he wrote, "I hope you will try to make arrangements for Jewell to join me as soon as possible. Her heart is with me. It is going to be much harder on her being here waiting for me than on me being there doing that which God has called us to do. I would appreciate anything you can do to expedite her return to China to join me."

John and his party sailed on June 6, 1944, a day remembered by history not as the date a small group of missionaries set forth on a freighter bound for China, but as the dáy Allied Troops crossed the English Channel and invaded Normandy. It was D-Day.

Two months later John lay uncomfortably on a bed soaked by his own sweat in a small hotel in Calcutta, India. Rising over him like a white shroud was the ubiquitous mosquito net. As far as he was concerned, it was like shutting the gate after the horse fled. His face was red, his eyes bloodshot, his temperature 103 degrees. He had dengue fever.

A jumble of things vied for attention in John's mind as he lay in the damp confines of his bed. Dengue fever, the result of the bite of a small zebra-striped mosquito, was only one of his frustrations. His visa into China had been turned down several times since his arrival in Calcutta. The Japanese had started a new offensive in South China and were pressing up the West River rapdily. The Baptist hospital in the city of Wuchow had been captured. What had become of Bill Wallace, the Southern Baptist missionary doctor there, was anybody's guess, and John had with him a large supply of medicines for Bill. All his plans seemed to be coming apart.

Missionaries he was planning to join in China were coming out of the country, some of them passing through Calcutta and not even aware he was there. Rex Ray, who had been with Bill Wallace, had reportedly passed through. If he could have seen Rex, he might have learned of Wallace's whereabouts.

Fever nagging him with thirst, he reached laboriously from under the net for the water bottle. As he drank the water, he prayed silently that he was not ingesting intestinal trouble. He had had more than his share of that since he arrived in India. Lying down wearily, he readjusted the mosquito net. John wondered if he had made a mistake in not accepting the army's offer made him the first week there.

When his visa was turned down by military authorities in Calcutta he was told of an opportunity to go into China as an interpreter with the rank of major in the American military. It was tempting. He had prayed through the night before he decided that he could do it only on the condition that he be allowed to go to his part of the country and do missionary work whenever he had an opportunity. The army could not surrender that much control. Now he wondered if he would ever get back to China.

Additional frustration was built around Jewell's inability to join him.

There had been only one high point. He had preached in the church at Serampore where William Carey, the father of the modern mission movement, began his work in 1792. It was a sacred moment. So impressed was he with the place where Carey had labored that, when he wrote Jewell of the event, he neglected to mention a visit to the Taj Mahal.

After John left for China, Jewell studied the accordion, spoke to far too many groups, and began still another project. At age fifty she learned to drive a car. She wrote a friend at the Foreign Mission Board: "The lady who took on the job of teaching me said, 'Now don't go more than twenty-five miles an hour.' It was the third day before I ever so much as saw the speedometer! The shift sounded like a threshing machine, but I got where I was going with many maneuvers. Oh, you fortunate children who learned without knowing it!"

Jewell prayed a lot. She knew and believed in the power of prayer.

She had seen too many miracles in China and in her own life to treat with anything less than the utmost seriousness the opportunity to lay her concerns, anxieties, and known needs before the Lord.

She prayed for Dr. Wallace, who was missing with the whole Wuchow hospital staff. She prayed that John would recover quickly from the fever, and asked God to open the door to China for him. Praying was a balm for the pain of not being with John. She knew he needed her. "He must be in agony," she said to a friend. "He needs to be about; he is so restless."

Yet, when the Japanese advance began, she was relieved that he was not in China. The time difference had bracketed anxious days.

In October she toured Oklahoma, speaking in schools of missions and finally to the state Woman's Missionary Union convention. When she returned to Arkansas, she found a cable. Tearing it open, she read: "Safe and well. In Kunming. John."

John staggered under the weight of two suitcases he carried across the ramp to the open door of the Army DC-3. He and five other missionaries who were a part of the liaison group with Dr. Price were finally going into China. The plane was to take them across "the Hump," as it was called—the magnificent Himalayas—to Kunming, one of the large cities still in Chinese hands.

As he started up the ramp, the man in front of him looked back and said, "This doesn't look like armistice day, does it?"

John looked around at the planes, the soldiers in khaki, and the gear. He grinned. "It surely doesn't."

It was November 11, 1944, before the trip to China that John began on June 6 looked as if it would finally be completed.

What bothered him most was the fact that six single women missionaries who had come out of China shortly ahead of him had gone right on in and become a part of the ministry at Kweilin before it was evacuated. His male ego suffered under the thought.

John, with very little experience in airplanes, felt his stomach tighten as the plane rumbled down the Calcutta runway, gaining speed for flight. Sitting back toward the tail section, he felt it rise, and then the ground began to recede below him. He looked at his companions and said wryly, "The only way to travel!"

They seemed even less assured than he.

All of them soon had their faces glued to the windows, taking in the magnificent panorama of the Himalayas. Later he wrote: "Beautiful scenery in the form of rugged mountains, forests, and jungles, peaks that came right up to the airplane, lights and shadows in the valleys, with changing cloud effects all the way. Then we were over the larger mountains and there was Mount Everest, towering above the clouds with its blanket of snow, shades of beautiful pastel colors of pink, purple, gray, and blue in the morning sunlight. I thanked God for his handiwork. Once seen, such things can never be forgotten."

The mountains gave way to foothills and signs of the familiar patterns of Chinese life. As the plane flew closer and closer to the ground, over small villages, roads, rice fields, and canals, John thought how fertile it was compared to Shantung. Before he knew it, the plane was rolling along the ground, safely down to China.

As John disembarked, he heard his name. Waving vigorously from the crowd was Dr. Greene Strother of the Southern Baptist Mission.

Strother said, "I want you to come with me to the church. Seeing a missionary arrive is going to be a welcome change for these people. All they have been doing lately is saying goodbye to missionaries."

"It's still that bad?" John asked.

"Well, the Japanese are still advancing, but I am not sure it is 'still that bad.' There seems to be some resistance, and a large number of troops and a lot of supplies have been moving in the other direction for a change."

As bad as the refugee problem had been in Shantung during the early days of the war, it was far worse in Kunming. John wrote Jewell, "Everything is in a chaotic state from the standpoint of the war and one cannot tell what will take place from one day to the next."

But John was sure God had led him there. He wrote, "There is no doubt in my mind but that he opened the way for me to return and has led me into a special kind of work where I can show forth my love and devotion to our Lord, serve the government in China and serve our own country at the same time."

Especially gratifying to John was the safe delivery to Greene Strother of the supply of medicines that had been entrusted to him. Strother was to make arrangements to move them on to Bill Wallace, who had appeared safely in Posei with his entire hospital staff. They were literally a hospital in transit, with staff, medicines, beds, and patients all in tow.

Within a few weeks, John bade his colleagues in Kunming goodbye and boarded a plane for flight to the Chinese wartime capital of Chungking. Just before he left, Greene Strother pressed a letter from Jewell into his hand.

"Guess what," she wrote, "the Board sent us a thousand dollars today to cover the things we lost in Shantung. They regretted that it was all they had, but I praise the Lord for it."

John had to laugh as he read it. A thousand dollars was not going to go very far in Chungking when a pound of butter cost 15,000 Chinese dollars. Of course, with a fairly favorable rate of exchange that was only seven dollars in U.S. money.

As the plane climbed into the clouds, John read the rest of her letter. She had been to Fort Worth, Texas, and had "sweet fellowship."

"I was a guest in the Culpepper-Glass households," she wrote. "The Connelys were with us to lunch, so we really had eight of the North China Mission. I requested that they have a business session and send me on to China."

He regretted he had not been able to write her before he boarded the plane, and resolved to write as soon as he got to Chungking. It looked as if Kunming would be evacuated, and he knew she would hear that on the radio before he could get any word to her. She has had a lot of worry with me, he thought.

In Chungking John found that he was in the Chinese army. He wore an officer's uniform with a special insignia to indicate that he was a liaison officer. His particular job was to teach English to young Chinese students who had been exposed to it before. In fact, some of them were Ph.D. graduates from United States universities. Many were Christians, and seemed excited when they found that John could share with them the Christian way of life.

Soon he was teaching the Chinese language to American troops in the area, English to Chinese troops, and preaching to and baptizing some of both.

Several times he met someone he had known in Shantung. Most were young men who had been pressed into service and had been retreating with the Chinese army for five years across the whole country. Some had more recent word from Shantung than he, and they brought him up to date on both the victories and the sufferings of the churches there.

Though he missed Jewell, he rejoiced that the Lord had brought him friends. Buford Nichols and Charles Culpepper were also wearing liaison officers' uniforms and carrying the same responsibilities as he.

The three of them felt that God had led them into the liaison service in order that they might remain in China. Other missionaries were being shunted out of the country by any transportation available. As liaison officers they were considered "essential."

News from other parts of the world was better than from China. In late February they heard that U. S. forces had recaptured Manila. In May the British took Rangoon. John wrote the Foreign Mission Board: "I see many sure signs that God is preparing the way for the greatest missionary effort the world has ever known in this land immediately following the war. The opportunities will be limited only by the number of missionaries and the means to keep them here. Now is the time for Southern Baptists to get ready for that new day."

The opportunity to serve as Christ's witness to his classes and to other refugees continued to expand. Authorized by his church in Fort Smith, Arkansas, to baptize new believers into their fellowship until they could find their own fellowship, John waded into the Chialing River one Sunday morning to baptize forty cadets. A large group of Christians lined the bank and sang throughout the service. Many boats passing by pulled over to watch the scene.

John wrote Jewell: "It was a happy day for us all. I am more convinced than ever, if that is possible, that soul-saving is the biggest job in the world. There is more joy in doing it than in anything else I have done."

An unusual opportunity began to develop for John and his colleagues to rub shoulders with men in high levels of both the American and Chinese governments. At a Fourth of July reception given by the American Embassy, John and Buford were invited as special guests and introduced to Ambassador Patrick Hurley and Lieutenant General Alfred Wedermeyer. Later John talked with one of the top Chinese generals. The general had been associated with communism for a while, but as he talked with him, John felt that he was rethinking his position. On a number of occasions the liaison officers were guests of Generalissimo and Madame Chiang Kai-shek.

In the midst of the most horrible news of the war came the most blessed. The horrible news came on August 6 and 9 with reports of the detonation of a new weapon called an atomic bomb over the Japanese cities of Hiroshima and Nagasaki. John read the accounts of it again and again, trying to comprehend what it meant: the number of dead, the horror, the radical change it made in everything.

A few days later, as John Abernathy and Buford Nichols came out from their classes, bells began to ring, sirens sounded, and streets filled with jubilant people. The war was over! Everybody was hugging everybody else. John reported: "I have never been hugged by so many people in all my life. You can't believe the joy that was everywhere.

"Tiny tots were crying out, 't'ou hsiang liao, t'ou hsiang liao' (surrendered, surrendered). China, the first to enter the war and the last to quit fighting, was free again. I caught the spirit and was yelling just like the rest of the Chinese and American soldiers."

Shortly after the war John and several other liaison officers were decorated with the order of the Cloud and Banner, the highest civilian decoration offered by the Chinese. Chiang Kai-shek greeted each one of them at the presentation. John had been the generalissimo's guest for religious services several times in his home.

Just before the end of the war John met Chiang's eldest son, Jing-kuo. The son had spent eight years as a student in Moscow and had become a staunch Communist. He married a Russian girl while there and had two children. He told John that all had changed.

"I am a Christian now," he said. "Not because someone preached to me. When I returned to China, I was living in a small house and was given the office of being chief of a county. One day my father visited me. After he left, I found this book on the table. I discovered it to be a Bible and resolved to burn it immediately. On the front flyleaf I saw something written with my father's signature at the bottom. There was still a spark of filial piety in my heart, and so I decided to read it for the 'old man's sake.' Many Scripture references were written, such as John 3:16, 3:5, and 3:36. I turned to these and read them. For some reason I could not stop and went on reading for a long time. I resolved to burn the book the next day, but the following morning I continued to examine it. I found eternal life through reading the Bible. After interpreting in Russian many passages to my wife, she also believed. We have led our children to acknowledge Christ."

John shared the experience with Jewell word for word in a long letter.

During a meeting arranged by American diplomats between Chiang Kai-shek and Communist leaders, John was introduced to Mao Tse-tung, leader of the Communist Party. In a letter to Rankin, John commented: "He was an impressive fellow, but I have deep suspicions about Communists. Not only because of their atheism, but because of what I fear they will do to China."

In Arkansas, Jewell was keeping the telephone and the mails busy with her efforts to get back to China. Her friend Rosalee Mills Appleby wrote: "Jewell had not stopped looking eastward. How she loved China, with its heathen pilgrimages and pagodas, its heavenly gates and dragon heads, its lotus lakes and rice paddies, its venerated burial mounds and sacred mountains. Jewell would close her eyes and see the peaceful trade caravans traveling the long roads of China more safely now. She envisioned the sacred mountains with multitudes climbing to their heights in search of soul satisfaction. Would the peace declared bring balm to a poor torn China?"

When John wrote Jewell that his contract time would soon be up and he would try to get to Tsinan, she redoubled her efforts. Her shouts filled the house when a letter arrived with news that she and two other missionary wives had approval to return to China.

Because of the strong surge of Chinese communism in North China immediately after the Japanese surrender, the question had been in doubt. Communists cut all railroads, highways, and telephone and telegraph connections. Before Central Government troops could be transported to the area, Communists took over the captured Japanese arms and firmly established themselves in a position of strength.

A letter came from John. It was posted from Tsinan. John was home. She rushed to complete her packing.

John completed his liaison duties on December 17 and, still in uniform, grabbed his baggage and went to the airport. Military style, he hopped the first plane going his way. Three and a half hours later he was in the city of Tsinan.

He was beseiged by friends as word spread that "Mr. Abernathy is back."

John said, "I left here June 16, 1942, a prisoner of the Japanese, and no Chinese dared accompany me to the train for fear of creating suspicion. What a change it was when I got back!"

John was greeted by the highest military official in Tsinan, Major General Li. Later he was taken to meet the governor. The governor said, "My house is your house."

But John had another house in mind. As soon as he could excuse himself, he jumped into the jeep that was made available to him and drove to the Baptist compound. Japanese troops were still in Tsinan, though they had put down their arms.

Parking the jeep in front of his house, which looked a bit worse for wear, John walked by the Japanese guard who saluted him smartly. John knocked at the door and was admitted by a Japanese houseboy. He asked for Colonel Kato.

In a moment the colonel walked into the room and stopped, as if seeing a ghost. Struggling to reproduce the exact words with which the colonel had evicted him four years earlier, John said, "Colonel, you have four days to leave my house. Take with you only the things you brought. Take nothing of mine."

The colonel said, "You are very generous. Four days will be quite enough. Thank you."

Then at the colonel's invitation John sat down and as the two shared tea, he shared with the colonel his faith in Jesus Christ. John's smugness in repossessing the house disappeared as he saw the colonel as a person for whom Christ died, a person who needed the love of God.

The next weeks were busy days. Not only did John hurry to refurnish the house for the return of his wife, but he endeavored to make contact with leaders of the churches. Daily he knelt in prayer with his reunited brethren. He was grateful beyond belief for the way they had prospered spiritually even while they suffered physically and materially. John realized that the great outpouring of love and spiritual power that God had granted them in the early 30s in what they now called the Shantung Revival had been his blessed way of preparing them for the trials that came.

Some had lost their lives. The stories that John listened to in the quiet of the Chinese homes as he shared meals with them moved him to tears.

Then one day he caught the train to Shanghai to meet Jewell's boat. Still in his uniform (he found that it opened doors that nothing else opened), he greeted his smiling wife for the first time in eighteen months. They held each other tightly before John said, "Let's go home."

A few hours later they stood like newlyweds in their home in Tsinan and looked around.

"We're home again, John," Jewell said.

He smiled. "Home again!" And then he added, "Now that you're here."

John's early return to Tsinan made him something of a folk hero among the Chinese. His military rank and familiarity with the governor placed him in a position to be of great help to them.

They needed all the help they could get. By spring of 1946 battles raged between Communist and Nationalist forces throughout Shantung Province. John was asked to head up relief work in the area. The people had suffered not only from the Japanese, but also from famine. Now they suffered deprivations imposed by the battle with Communists.

Late in 1946 John himself ran into a battle. He with an American military officer drove a jeep toward one of the villages where relief operations were being projected. Suddenly they heard the popping of guns all around them.

"Turn around, John, quick!" the officer shouted.

A bullet shattered the windshield even as he spoke. John slammed on the brakes, jumped from the jeep, and crouched behind it. More bullets came. When the shooting stopped, John raised up. He felt whoozey. He looked at his companion whose face was ashen.

"My god, John, you're hit!" the American officer exclaimed.

John raised his hand to the back of his neck and pulled it away bright red. Blood was flowing copiously from a wound behind his ear. It quickly soaked his collar and the front of his tunic. Despite the officer's efforts to stop the bleeding, blood was soon running out from John's sleeve and off the ends of his fingers. He leaned heavily against the hood of the damaged jeep. Is this how it feels to go? he thought, feeling life rush from him.

Quietly he prayed, "Lord, if this is where it ends, it's all right with me. I am in your hands. If you have more for me to do, then you will have to save me, but I am in your hands."

Hearing a shuffling down the bank, he turned, expecting to see Communist soldiers coming to finish the job. Instead through glazed eyes he saw a Nationalist Army corpsman running toward him with a first-aid kit.

"The only seriousness to the wound is the bleeding," the corpsman informed John as he completed a bandage. "Had I not come, you might well have died. Now you will get well quickly."

"Man, were you ever lucky!" his military companion commented. John just smiled. He knew better. Evidently, God had more for him to do.

John's feelings against communism grew stronger as everywhere he went he saw its misery. Strife and turmoil and fear seemed to follow the Red tide. He wrote Baker J. Cauthen: "In sections where they rule, everything that is right has been upset. Home life, the virtue of womanhood, filial piety, religion, etc., have all been done away with as far as the Communists are concerned. A person having over two acres of land is branded a 'capitalist,' is arrested, publicly humiliated, stripped of everything, and sent away to beg. In some places churches have been closed and Christians scattered."

In a rush of feeling he added: "We may have to deal with Russia later, but the sooner communism is eradicated from the earth, the sooner we shall have peace. You may think that sounds unchristian, but it is not, and comes from one who knows and loves everyone of China's 450,000,000 souls. The sooner America gets her eyes open to the facts and uses her efforts to save China from communism, the sooner she will prove her interest and friendship for the people here."

John was frustrated by American efforts to work out a compromise between Chiang and Mao. "It will never work," he said over and over again to Jewell. "It's either right now or it will soon be all over."

The scope of his feelings surprised him, but there they were.

7
Red Tide

For John and Jewell Abernathy, the days following the surrender of the Japanese, were hectic. Reluctant as they were to admit it, the longed-for peace, a dream that sustained them through the war years, seemed as elusive as ever. Communism was pressing closer like a Red tide sweeping in, and the sound of guns could be heard on the borders of the city. Then things would grow quiet as another round began at the conference table.

The church work flourished. Jewell recommenced her Bible schools for women. The mission schools were reopened with both John and Jewell teaching and John serving as principal. The churches throughout the countryside bearing the brunt of violence and hardships needed a great deal of help and encouragement. Whenever the Communists pulled back, John and Jewell ventured out to these churches to teach and encourage.

Their efforts were facilitated by John's involvement with the authorities in Tsinan. Governor Wang seemed especially interested in him, seeking his advice and counsel and sending him on a number of relief-related missions.

During a difficult period in the early days of the Communist threat, Tsinan and Tsingtao were the only cities in Shantung Province that were neither occupied by the Communists nor besieged. The menaced cities included Taian, where John and Jewell originally began their missionary career, and Liaocheng, southwest of Tsinan. In the spring, UNRRA, the relief arm of the United Nations, tried to move a large supply of food to the beleagured citizens of Liaocheng. The Communists had cut off all roads and railroads leading to them and the people were literally starving to death.

Governor Wang asked John if he would serve on a team to lead ten UNRRA trucks of food into the besieged city. The team was to include an American colonel, a Nationalist colonel, a Communist major, and an American sergeant. The Chinese version of UNRRA was to be represented by two Chinese and John Abernathy.

John rode in the lead jeep when the caravan pulled out of Tsinan shortly after 5 o'clock in the morning. Roads were bad and breakdowns frequent. They were still in Nationalist territory by evening. Early the next morning, after spending the night in spartan quarters, the Communist major, Kao, and John drove ahead in one of the jeeps. To their surprise, they were unable to make contact with any of the Communist troops.

Coming to a deep ditch that had been refilled to allow traffic to cross the road, they decided to wait there for the trucks to catch up. When the trucks approached, John's jeep passed slowly over the fill, and the trucks began to follow. The first truck passed over all right, but the second sank up to its axles in the fill. The convoy ground to a halt.

All the drivers were pressed into service around the stalled vehicle. When they had surrounded the truck and put their shoulders to it to push, a shot rang out. The group stood up and looked around to discover that they were completely surrounded by a large bank of Communist soldiers. A few more shots were fired, evidently a warning to convoy men scrambling for cover. Soon the group were herded with hands behind their heads into a building at the side of the road. A communist official, not in uniform, began to swear at them for invading Communist territory without proper credentials. John, with his hands clasped behind his head, replied that was not so. He turned to the Communist Major Kao, but the official said Major Kao was a spy.

After some argument and a great deal of poking around in the trucks, they were allowed to proceed with a Communist soldier attached to the party. Late that evening they arrived at the suburbs of Liaocheng.

John and Major Kao were again in the lead jeep. They were about a half mile ahead of the convoy. As they drove to a roadblock, Communist soldiers stepped from the darkness and Major Kao and John got out of the jeep and greeted them.

John prayed silently that they weren't "trigger-happy." John explained their business and showed them his papers. The Communists agreed to admit the party. John and Major Kao got back into their jeep and started back to the trucks. They had gone no more than a few yards when the major asked John to stop the jeep. He said he was tired and would go into town to make arrangements for a place for them to stay. It was the last John ever saw of Major Kao.

When the relief convoy reached the roadblock, they were greeted warmly by the Communists and taken to a sumptuous meal. After the meal John asked when they could distribute the food. The Communist colonel replied that it would be impossible because the general in charge was away and he was the only one who could give permission. When they tried to leave, John realized they were prisoners.

Early the next morning the Communist colonel awakened the party and told them he was going to search the trucks and wanted them present. Bayonets were stuck into the milk tins. John and the other leaders protested as the precious liquid poured out on the ground, but they were warned not to interfere. The same thing happened to the flour.

"We have information," the colonel explained, "that you are trying to smuggle arms and ammunitions into the city."

"We have no such items," John said.

A large sum of money in the manifest for payrolls was found and confiscated.

Finally, the team leaders were allowed to go into the city empty-handed. They explained their difficulty to the officials. A number of negotiating efforts were made, but they were futile. The Communist commander was adamant.

After the last effort the team was not even allowed to go into the city. It was obvious they had lost everything.

John was a discouraged liaison officer when he returned to Tsinan to report to the governor. His experience embittered him regarding America's efforts to strike a coalition between the Communists and the Nationalists.

"It'll never work," John told Jewell. "The Communists want all or nothing, and they don't intend to get nothing."

That night they lay awake talking in muted tones about John's experience.

"The thing that bothers me most, Jewell," John said, "is the faces of those starving people. To think that food was just outside the gate."

Jewell said, "It's ironic, isn't it? Our Chinese people are suffering more under the Chinese Communists than they did under the Japanese."

Despite the uncertainty, throughout 1946 and 1947 the Southern Baptist Foreign Mission Board strenghtened Missions in China. John and Jewell entertained new missionaries coming through, supervised rebuilding efforts, and trained Chinese workers. In addition to the new missionaries, they were strengthened by a large number returning. Many had been out of China since 1941.

By the spring of 1948, the Abernathys were wondering if the chaotic state of affairs would ever change, either for better or for worse. For worse seemed more likely. Railroad tracks were torn up between Tsinan and other major cities. Regular plane service was cancelled off. Prices continued to rise, and many commodities were not to be had.

Chiang Kai-shek moved new troops into the area to guarantee the security of Tsinan, and spent several days in the city. John, as a confidant of the governor, was invited to meet with the generalissimo, along with the U.S. consul and several military advisors.

Two weeks later, however, the U. S. consul at Tsingtao advised all Americans in Tsinan to evacuate to Tsingtao. They expected Communists to make an all-out effort to take the city.

"Seems like we've heard that before." said Jewell.

Two days after that, three American C46 planes landed at Tsinan, expecting to remove the twenty-eight Americans. Only three boarded the plane. Thirteen Germans, Australians, Spanish, and British personnel left, but the Americans wanted to stay. The three who left had been imprisoned by the Japanese during all the war and needed a furlough badly.

There was good news, too, John reported the Bible school filled to capacity. The Tsinan church basement was being utilized by a high school refugeeing from Liaocheng. Another part of the building housed a college of political science which had been hastily pulled together to counteract intensive Red propaganda.

In some ways 1947 and 1948 were two of John and Jewell's best years in China. John, serving as an advisor to the governor of Shantung, was named an honarary member of the legislature. He attended every major event held.

On a number of occasions he tried to witness about Christ to the governor and wrote Dr. Cauthen in November 1947 that he thought the governor was "not far from the kingdom."

In early 1948 John was appointed a major general in the Chinese army. This was a promotion from his liaison rank of colonel and was based on his relief work and the service he rendered the governor.

Early the same year the Foreign Mission Board notified John and Jewell they would be eligible for furlough in May, since John had returned to China during the war.

"John, I hate to go," Jewell said. "We've never had more doors open to us. We have no way of knowing what will happen while we are gone."

"I know," John replied. He also had an uneasy feeling about leaving.

He had just come from a visit with Japanese war criminals awaiting execution by the Nationalist government. Two had professed faith in Christ. He had also arranged with the governor to have access to Communist prisoners interned outside Tsinan.

"I feel sure many of them will be open to the gospel," John wrote in a letter to Cauthen and added, "I guarantee you, if they become Christians, their stomach for communism will disappear."

The Foreign Mission Board continued to send missionaries into China, but so much of North China was under Communist control that many of the missionaries who would ordinarily have served elsewhere were assigned to Tsinan. It fell to John to develop quarters and work opportunities for them.

Just before John and Jewell left for furlough, the Frank Connelys and Charles Culpeppers came for a visit. They reminisced at length about the days of the Shantung revival, life under the Japanese, and other high and low moments they had shared.

It was a strange situation. Missionaries who had been in the United States since the beginning of the Chinese-Japanese war were coming in even as missionaries who had been driven from Communist areas were beginning to go out, frightened and discouraged by what they had seen.

In the Abernathy household, tones grew hushed as exiting missionaries told of public trials, executions, intimidations, and Christian martyrs. John's bitterness toward communism, fed by his fear of what it would do to his beloved China, grew.

Yet he tried to "think positively," as Jewell said, and the results in Tsinan helped. Over a hundred professions of faith in one of the Tsinan churches during January of 1948 was an example of the kind of response that was marking their postwar tenure.

In March they received word from the Foreign Mission Board that reservations had been made for them on the USS *General Meigs* to return in May for furlough.

As they packed, they were interrupted time and again by calls from the governor to help greet the steady stream of American diplomats and army officers who came through Tsinan to contact both Communist and Nationalist leaders in an effort to work out some kind of coalition government. An uneasy peace held while the negotiations continued.

Thus, when John and Jewell shipped their bags to Shanghai for the trip home, they nursed genuine hope that a year later they would return to an improved situation. Even before they boarded the ship, all that changed. Negotiations broke down, and word came of heavy Communist attacks on Nationalist positions.

During the voyage home, they were preoccupied with the news. One village where Baptists had work was reported captured by the Communists. Before they arrived in Fort Smith for their furlough residence, they began to wonder if they would ever get back to China. Had the sad and thoughtful Chinese who bade them farewell known deep in their souls they were saying a final goodbye to their friends of so many years?

When John returned to their Fort Smith apartment from a trip to the post office on September 26, Jewell had laid out their noon meal in the sunny little breakfast nook.

"Hey, you got here just in time," she said, leading the way to the table. "Any mail from China?"

"Two letters!" John answered. "One from Jenny Alderman and another from Pastor Tong, neither one very encouraging."

He sat down at the table with Jewell. It seemed strange to have food enough to cause worry about their weight, but between America's plenty and their propensity to gain, the Abernathys ate with care.

John asked the blessing, listing names and concerns that had come with the two letters. As they began to eat, John reached over and turned on the radio to get the noon news broadcast. The lead story ruined their appetites.

"Chiang Kai-shek reported this morning that the key Shantung city of Tsinan has fallen to the Communists."

The news of the next few days nearly broke their hearts. Governor Wang had been captured and killed. Reports about missionaries still there were initially reassuring, but a lack of real news, along with a deep distrust of anything mediated through the Communists, left John and Jewell uneasy.

They carried heavy speaking schedules during the fall. By Christmas they realized that their chance of returning to Tsinan was very remote. John lobbied all he could for America to help Chiang Kai-shek's faltering government in any way possible.

"Don't let China fall to the Communists," he said again and again as he encouraged prayer on behalf of Chiang's government.

Privately he and Jewell considered where else they might serve. Formosa (now Taiwan) was a possibility. West China where John served as liaison worker was another if the Nationalists could halt the Red tide.

A Washington group called the China Emergency Committee invited John to come to the capital in March to address a group of businessmen and Congressmen on his missionary experience in China, including his contact with the Communists. Congressman Walter Judd, and Baptist pastor, C. W. Cranford, issued the invitation.

On the way to Washington, John stopped off at the Foreign Mission Board's headquarters in Richmond, Virginia, to get any late word concerning the missionaries behind Communist lines. New peace talks were being carried on between the Communist and National governments, but he doubted their effectiveness.

"I've seen that before," he said. "That simply means the Reds are waiting for more supplies."

Missionaries trying to stay in Communist lands were now discouraged. More and more of them were coming out. Rumor was that the United States was going to send ships to North China to remove American civilians still there.

What John learned in Washington was not encouraging either.

"Too little, too late," he said to Jewell in summing it all up.

Approximately a month later John recieved word from one of his Presbyterian missionary friends detailing the fall of Tsinan. The missionary wrote: "I hope I never have to live through another five days like the . . . five were. We were thoroughly looted—shelled from both sides—but no one of our staff was killed or injured. I believe the same holds true for all the Christian organizations in the city.

"I visited your Mission compound twice. A battery was operated from there, and I counted 150 graves in the yards surrounding your houses."

This really upset John and Jewell because they had left over a hundred refugees access to their compound until they returned from furlough. Many of these must have died during the battle.

Their friend reported that CAT (Cathay Air Transport) planes had landed and taken off right up until the Communists took over.

"There were people actually hanging to the wings and falling off on the take-off run," he wrote. "But the early stages were not bad. There was some order and no repression."

John had seen that happen in other areas taken over by the Communists. He was pessimistic about the long-term possibilities. He had talked to too many missionaries who had tried to work under Communist domination.

"It starts off all sweetness and light," one had said, "but suddenly they begin to put the screws to you."

By the time the Southern Baptist Convention rolled around in May, John and Jewell knew they would not be using the return part of their ticket to China. They began consultations in the early fall of 1949 about another place to work.

Their uncertainty was eased by a busy deputation schedule. Jewell spoke to groups of women in Maryland, in Washington, D.C., and in Virginia, as John spoke in Arkansas and Tennessee. Then John went to Mobile, Alabama, for a speaking engagement where he also rendezvoused with the Foreign Mission Board's executive secretary, Dr. Rankin. Over coffee, Rankin shared a new development with him.

"I received a good letter from Baker Cauthen in Hong Kong last week," Rankin said.

John stirred his coffee. He knew Cauthen, the Orient secretary, had been forced to move his headquarters from Shanghai to Hong

Kong because of the Communist advance.

"I hope they're well," John responded.

Dr. Rankin nodded. "Doing very well. He introduced a possibility for you and Jewell that I want to talk with you about."

John had discussed with the secretary during the summer the possibility of going to Africa. Neither he nor Jewell felt the Lord's leadership in it despite the opportunities outlined.

"Why don't we go to Hawaii?" Jewell had said. Ever since her visit there before Pearl Harbor, she had had a strong interest in the islands with their representative group of Asians.

"We would be half-way to China if the opportunity opens up for us to go on back there," she added with a twinkle in her eye.

"Now the real reason comes out," John had kidded her.

"What did Cauthen suggest?" John asked Rankin.

"Korea."

John looked up with interest, "Korea?"

In all his years in China, he had not been far from Korea. The ancient Asian peninsula was just across the Yellow Sea from Shantung Province, but he had never been there. He had known it to be the scene of heroic Christian activity since the turn of the century. He also knew it had been the location of a dramatic revival even before Shantung's revival in the early 30s.

There was controlled excitement in John's voice. "Tell me some more."

"Baker and Ed Dozier of Japan made a trip over there about two months ago," Dr. Rankin told him, "in response to a letter we had from a group of Christians who thought they were Baptists and wanted to make contact with us."

"They *thought* they were Baptists!" John said, puzzled.

Dr. Rankin smiled, "They haven't called themselves Baptists through the years. They are the product of an American missionary named Fenwick who went to Korea around the turn of the century He was sponsored by the Boston church pastored by A. J. Gordon. But from what this group knows about Baptists, they think they are Baptists."

Rankin told him that Cauthen and Dozier, a missionary to Japan, had met with these Christians who survived the Japanese occupation for twenty years at great cost and with many martyrs. Cauthen said it was like seeing a group of people walking into the light and blinking. Because many of the people speak Japanese as a result of the long Japanese occupation, Dozier went along to translate for Cauthen.

"I thought the Koreans didn't like the Japanese," John remarked.

"How right you are!" said Rankin. "In fact, Baker began to speak and Dozier to translate into Japanese when one of the Korean men stood up and stopped him with 'Not another word! We do not intend to listen to Japanese ever again.'

"Fortunately, Baker found one in the group who spoke Chinese."

Later, several Korean leaders who could speak English joined them, and communication was eased somewhat.

"That gives you something of the spirit of these people," Rankin said.

"Baker outlined to them who Southern Baptists are and what they believe. The Korean Christians said, 'Well, that's who we are.'

"Baker asked them to think about it and pray about it and wire him. They wired him, 'Korean Baptist Convention just organized. Send missionaries.' "

Rankin looked at Abernathy intently, trying to read his thoughts. John was definitely interested.

It was Cauthen's idea to approach Abernathy, Rankin added. He reasoned that John's proven ability to work with all strata of society uniquely equipped him. "He can relate to peasants and princes with equal ease," Cauthen had written Rankin. "The highest military and civilian powers in China asked his confidence. Within the poorest villages he was welcomed as a brother."

"Besides," Cauthen continued, "John and Jewell are both rugged people. They have pioneering ability, and this is going to be a pioneering situation."

Before John and Rankin separated in Mobile, Rankin thought he had his answer.

"I'll go home and tell Jewell to pack while I pray about it," John said smiling.

At the end of 1949 John and Jewell Abernathy were preparing feverishly for their return to the Orient. Everything they owned was in Communist hands in Tsinan. They were starting over again for the third time, the Japanese having carried off most of the first household ensemble.

Cauthen wrote them to contact a Mr. and Mrs. David Ahn when they got to Seoul. David Ahn, who had been like a son to the great missionary Fenwick, was one of the key leaders of the newly formed Korean Baptist Convention. His charm and abilities had been primarily responsible for convincing Cauthen of an opportunity for service in Korea.

"Mr. Ahn said you would probably be able to rent a house after you get there, but you should plan on staying at the Chosen Hotel in Seoul until you do," Cauthen wrote.

Chosen, John knew, was the Oriental name for Korea. It was also called the "Land of the Morning Calm." From what he read, he was not sure how calm it would be.

The country had been divided at the 38th parallel, the line at which the Japanese surrendered. The northern part came under Russian influence and the southern part came under American support. A democracy had been formed in the South with Syngman Rhee, a veteran of underground wars against the Japanese and later imprisoned by the Japanese, elected the first president.

But even as John and Jewell made their plans to go to Korea, the Communists north of the 38th parallel were making threatening gestures toward the South.

A major concern for the Abernathys was the difficult Korean language. They had become proficient in Chinese. Starting over again would be difficult.

"Don't worry, John. We got along quite well with the Koreans who lived in Tsinan, and they told us that many Koreans speak Chinese," Jewell reasoned.

"That's true," said John. "And I know that large communities of Chinese live in Seoul and in Pusan. We'll undoubtedly have an opportunity to minister to them as well as to Koreans. But you know how important it is to be able to speak the language of the country.'"

Jewell sighed. She knew. But God knew, also, and he was the one leading them to Korea.

They stopped off in Japan, flying from Tokyo to Fukuoka for conferences with Edwin Dozier and his wife Mary Ellen, before going on to Seoul. The Doziers had been in Japan before the war and were the first missionaries back. Dozier had served ably in Hawaii during the war. Dozier's father was a pioneer missionary among Southern Baptists in Japan.

After their brief visit with the Doziers, the Abernathys flew on to Seoul where they were told that Mr. Ahn, Pastor Kim, and others would meet them. Their excitement was high as the plane circled the Seoul airport for a landing.

"Why, look how big it is!" Jewell exclaimed, as they surveyed the sprawling city of two million. "It makes Tsinan look very small."

"It is a big city," said John. "I wonder what kind of welcome we'll have."

John didn't have to wait long to find out. As they got off the plane in Seoul and cleared customs, they walked into a waiting room packed with people greeting other people. John looked left and right and then looked at Jewell. No one was there to meet them.

Slowly they began to smile at each other.

"Welcome to the mission field, Jewell," John said.

"Thank you," Jewell replied, making a little curtsy.

Later, from their hotel room at the Chosen, they made contact with an embarrassed Mr. Ahn.

"Pastors from all the Baptist churches are in Seoul especially to greet you, but they didn't know your arrival time," he apologized.

Soon Mr. Ahn with his beautiful and talented wife arrived at the hotel to greet them effusively and introduce them to the Korean Baptist leaders. Each one, it seemed as Mr. Ahn talked, had a personal history not unlike that of the apostle Paul. By the time the Abernathys finally got to bed that first night in Korea, they realized how greatly they had been blessed by this assignment. They were entering into fellowship with a group of Christ's disciples who had been tempered, tried, and found true in great tribulation.

Strangers in a strange land, talking quietly of their greeting and what it meant, they thanked the Lord for bringing them to Korea.

"You know what I'm thinking, John?" Jewell asked.

"You're probably thinking the same thing I am," John answered.

"If you're thinking about Mr. Chao, I am," Jewell said.

"Yes," John said softly, "I was thinking of Mr. and Mrs. Chao and the children."

A few months before they left Tsinan, a little Korean woman appeared at their door. She said her husband had been pressed into service by the Japanese and was being held as a prisoner of war. John and Jewell tried to get her to return to Korea with her children on a repatriation train that was being set up by Governor Wang.

"No," she said, "I cannot. Not with my husband in a Chinese prison camp."

A few days later, Mrs. Chao's twelve-year-old daughter came to Jewell and asked, "Can I do your moving about?"

It dawned on Jewell that the child wanted to be her personal maid.

Jewell patiently explained that she had never used a maid servant, but that she would try to find a place for her to work.

Meanwhile, John visited Mr. Chao in prison, and talked to Governor Wang about a pardon. No stay in execution was possible. Mr. Chao was executed a few days later.

A letter from a Japanese cellmate of Mr. Chao's came to John shortly afterward: "Mr. Chao Yuan T'ah, a Korean, was led to Christ by you, and his survivors were placed under your affectionate charity. So we his Japanese friends want to heartily thank you."

John and Jewell had seen Mrs. Chao on her way to Korea.

Now they, too, were in Korea. Just before they went to sleep, Jewell asked, "Was it a prelude, John, an introduction?"

Their early days in Korea were full: visiting, meeting new people, counseling, preaching, attending meetings in strange places, sleeping on hot floors—the Korean way of handling the harsh winters that are a part of its climate—and eating the hot, spicy food, much stronger than they were used to in Shantung.

These were sensitive days, too. It was the beginning of a work with promise, and important precedents were being set. Requests came for considerable sums of money for large projects. The new Baptists dreamed of schools, hospitals, and a seminary. They desired attractive church buildings. They had been a despised minority for altogether too many years. John knew that many of them expected these dreams to materialize with their relationship to Southern Baptists.

Even more delicate was a split within their own ranks between two leaders. The man who had invited Cauthen to Korea was a Dr. Wu, who had been in the United States as a young Christian attending the Southern Baptist Theological Seminary at Louisville, Kentucky. When he returned to Korea, he was unable to locate a Baptist group as such, and he attached himself to the group which had grown up around Wonsan in North Korea under the ministry of Dr. Fenwick.

Sometime later, the Japanese arrested twenty of their leaders for teaching Christ's second coming in a way that indicated Christ must be greater than the emperor. The leaders were questioned at length and imprisoned. Some died. John learned that Dr. Wu was accused of the indiscretion that led to their imprisonment. Yet it was Dr. Wu who had contacted Southern Baptists and Cauthen. Mr. Ahn, John's host and a man of great charm, was very distrustful of Dr. Wu. The Abernathys were greatly impressed by the Ahns.

Jewell wrote: "Mrs. Ahn is one of the loveliest people I have ever known. She goes everywhere with me and interprets for me. I have never spoken through an interpreter like her. She even interprets my gestures. As far as I can tell, she doesn't miss a nuance. And she is always out in front of me anticipating any needs I might have. Really, I am afraid I am going to be totally spoiled."

John felt the same way about Mr. Ahn. When the housing that had been promised proved unavailable, it was the Ahns who opened their home to the Abernathys.

John was compelled to walk a fragile line between the factions. He tried to help the new Baptists understand what Baptists in the rest of the world were like. But unlike Baptists in most places, Korean Baptists had elders, as well as pastors and deacons. After hearing John describe Baptist polity and practice in other parts of the world, they voted to eliminate elders and have only pastors and deacons.

In May 1950, John and Jewell journeyed to Juhmchon, where a church with nearly four hundred members was located, for the first meeting of the Korean Baptist Convention. They arrived at Juhmchon by train and were greeted not only by official delegates from the church, but also by most of the members and, it seemed to John, the rest of the town.

He wrote Cauthen, "We walked from the station to the home of Deacon Kim where we were to be entertained. So many people followed us that it was almost like a street parade."

At that meeting, Korean Baptists voted to begin educational and hospital work and urged Southern Baptists to send as many missionaries as possible. John guided them the best he could, trying to give tactful advice in a way that would not destroy the healthy indigenous aspect of the group. He tried to head off a tendency to regard alliance with the Foreign Mission Board as some kind of gold mine.

The Koreans' experience with American soldiers who came into their country following the Japanese war was most favorable. John and Jewell inherited that goodwill and found that it provided a great opportunity for Christian witness.

After the convention in Juhmchon, they went by train to Pusan to take possession of a new car and new furniture. Back in Seoul they positioned the furniture in the rooms the Ahns made available to them. As Jewell made the last adjustment to the last chair, she stood back and said, "Okay, John, here we go again. This is the third time we have outfitted ourselves. How long do you think this will last?"

John didn't have the heart to tell her he wasn't as optimistic as he had been a few weeks earlier. While in Pusan he had been briefed by military officers he had known in Chungking. They said North Korea's Communist government was making more trouble along the 38th parallel. The officers thought Russia and China were egging the North Koreans along, feeling that if they took over South Korea they would eliminate American influence in that part of Asia for good.

But John didn't tell Jewell that. Instead, he hugged her and laughed as he said, "Easy come, easy go."

Whatever came, he knew she could handle it.

Spring in Korea was a beautiful time. Sculptured hills, in size very much like the Appalachian Mountains in which John grew up, but supporting much less vegetation, dominated the countryside. Delicate green terraced slopes planted with rice could be seen in every direction.

Jewell noticed mothers with babies draped in brightly colored quilts across their backs and water jars or other heavy loads balanced on their heads.

It was familiar and unfamiliar. As in China, the people dressed in a combination of Western and traditional clothing. The traditional clothing was bulky, warm, and loosely flowing.

Like the peasants in China, Korean Jija men carried immense loads. Jewell knew they probably started as small children, working up as they grew older to increasingly larger burdens. The weight they could carry was unbelievable. Their new friends constantly greeted them with bouquets of flowers. One of Jewell's favorites was the purple rose azalea. Weeping willows were plentiful. Apricot trees gently shed pink blossoms before the spring winds that brushed over the hills and into the valleys, driving away the last chill of winter.

John and Jewell were astounded by the commitment of the churches with which they were assigned to work in the new missionary endeavor. That faith dominated their existence was obvious to John when he visited a church in Seven Hills. He went there one day in late spring with the pastor, a man named Lee. The church had only a small chapel. When John preached there was not enough room, so they had an open-air meeting. Later John walked into a room where the leaders were gathered and noticed that the floor was covered with food stuffs. He saw an old New York *Times* laying in a corner with blood all over it.

"What's this?" John asked.

Lee said, "These are the tithes of our people. In those bags is one tenth of the newly threshed rice. In the baskets are a tenth of the eggs gathered this week. Inside that old newspaper is a tenth of a pig butchered this past week."

During John's visit the people decided to build a larger building. They divided the task between male and female. The women would buy the land and the men would build it. They decided that each family would put a large stone jar beside the family rice jar. When a meal was cooked, a double handful of rice would be placed first of all in the Lord's jar. When the jar was full, it would be sold and the money laid aside.

They soon had enough money to buy the land.

Providing dirt from their rice fields, the men made adobe bricks from the dirt, chaff, and mortar. The walls began to go up, but they had no money to buy beams and rafters, so they prayed about it. John paid them another visit during the building and went back to Seoul amazed.

He said to Jewell, "There is temendous spiritual vitalty among these people—dedication beyond anything I have seen before. We've got a great opportunity ahead of us."

But their hopes began to unravel. After an exhausting trip to the mountain area, they lay abed until almost time for church on Sunday, June 27, 1950. Dressing hurriedly, they attended the 11 o'clock service in Seoul and returned to a delicious Sunday dinner prepared for them by the Ahns. At 4:30 they started for the English service at the Union Church, where they were developing contacts with other missionaries and receiving some personal spiritual food. On the way they noticed large crowds in the streets.

John tried to stop a Korean man in the crowd.

"What is it?" he asked in the few Korean words he knew.

The man explained carefully to him in Korean. John didn't understand a word of it.

Jewell saw an American missionary near the church.

"What's going on?" she inquired.

The man replied, "North Korean troops attacked across the 38th parallel this morning. It looks bad. A number of missionaries have been captured in one of the first battles."

By dark the streets were full of trucks loaded with soldiers heading north. One soldier explained to a Korean young person that he was going into battle. The youngster began to jump around saying, "Great! We will soon be back home in the North. Our troops will now unite all of Korea."

As the Ahns, who had joined them, interpreted the exchange to John and Jewell they watched the faces of the boy's elders. It was obvious that they didn't share the boy's confidence. When John and Jewell retired that night, they could hear the guns outside the city. They prayed a long time, holding up their newly adopted people in prayer and asking for confidence. The Lord gave them the Scripture, "He giveth his beloved sleep."

Cannon fire wasn't new to them. They had been through it in China. They had lived through the torturous days when the Japanese crossed China. They had lived through the devastation of conflict between Communist and Nationalist Chinese. Cannon fire was something they had heard before.

John and Jewell Abernathy weren't children whose pulse ran away each time they heard the sound of man's violence. What else did they expect from the world? They were there to represent the Man of Peace.

John turned out the light and they went to sleep.

At 3 A.M. a frantic knocking came at their door. It was Mr. Ahn. He announced that an evacuation was being planned for all Americans.

By the time they finished their breakfast, they were informed that most American women and children had been evacuated during the night. They decided to go to the church.

The Koreans were surprised to see them and asked, "When will you leave?"

John reassured them, "We have no plans yet. It's in the Lord's hands."

Despite a lot of advice, most of it urging them to leave, they prepared to spend the night again. But before dawn, an American consulate representative came to the Ahn house to inform the Abernathys that the last planes would be leaving at dawn.

"Your wife must be there if she is to go at all," he warned. "She will be allowed sixteen pounds of luggage. She has two hours."

"I'll talk to her," John said, "but she will make the decision."

Jewell heard John out, then she said simply, "No, I don't want to go."

They went back to sleep, but were awakened at dawn by planes flying low overhead, followed by explosions terrifyingly near. A telephone call came at breakfast. It was the consulate.

"We are closing and evacuating. There is no transportation left for you, so if you are coming, you will have to get to the field on your own."

John made up his mind. It wasn't up to his wife. "Pack a few things," he said. "We're leaving as soon as we can get off."

Within an hour they were on their way with a few hastily packed suitcases. David Ahn drove them to the airport, bade them a sad goodbye, and then drove back to care for his own family.

At 1 P.M. Jewell was placed on a plane with women and children, but was allowed to take only one suitcase. She picked one with the things she would need that night, gave John a hasty kiss, and boarded the plane.

John watched the plane soar off to the south and prayed it would not be intercepted by fighter planes now strafing the main city of Seoul. He picked up the remaining luggage and took it with him to a corner to await his own fate.

At 5 P.M. another plane arrived and John's number was called. As he started to get his baggage, the American airman supervising the evacuation said, "Forget it. This is a people flight. No baggage is allowed."

The explosions nearby and trucks with fleeing soldiers, many of them severely wounded, said even more about the situation. South Korean defenses had completely collapsed.

John climbed on the plane wondering what would happen to their things at the Ahns. He had been this way before, however, and things were not too important. Besides, he had a funny feeling about all that furniture, those clothes, and the car when he got them.

The plane landed in Fukuoka a few hours later and John found Jewell waiting patiently for him, looking only slightly the worse for wear.

"Well," she said as they embraced, "that was one of our shorter separations."

John wiped a tear from her eye, and said, "Let's be grateful for little things."

The two of them found a chance to minister to their fellow refugees. They learned long ago that such times provided the best opportunities to be the Lord's messengers.

Later, John found a moment to send a telegram to Baker Cauthen in Hong Kong: "Safe in Japan. No baggage. No bullet holes. Abernathy."

8
KOREA

On June 27, 1950, the United Nations entered the war against North Korea in an effort to halt the North's furious drive to bring all Korea under a Communist regime. Both South Korea and the United Nations had been pressing for unification through democratic elections, but observers had not been allowed to cross the 38th parallel into the North. The reason why was now evident: the Communists had their own unification plan.

John and Jewell were heartsick at the realization that the people they had come to love in just a few short weeks were once again suffering the ravages of war and occupation. They had no word from the Ahns and no way of knowing whether their Korean cohorts stayed in Seoul or fled before the advance.

By late August South Korean forces and the United Nations defenders, mostly American troops from the occupation forces under MacArthur in Japan, had been pushed back into a small perimeter north and west of Pusan.

At that same time, the Abernathys boarded a boat in Yokohama bound for Manila in the Philippines. Baker Cauthen, returning to the Orient from a furlough in the United States, had met with John in Tokyo. They decided that the Abernathys had three options: (1) to wait in Japan until the situation in Korea stabilized; (2) to go to Formosa (now Taiwan) where Bertha Smith from Shantung had begun a new work and was calling for help; or (3) to go to the Philippines.

They decided on the Philippine Islands for several reasons. Newly appointed Southern Baptist missionaries who had gone to China in 1948 and been driven out of language school in Peiping when the Communists took over had been sent to the Philippines to continue their study of Chinese. The language school had been established in Baguio, a lovely city nestled in the mountains on the island of Luzon. Also, several hundred thousand Chinese lived in the Philippines, and John and Jewell thought they could minister to the Chinese there until they found new opportunities. When bad news continued to come out of China, the idea of permanent work among the Chinese in the Philippines seemed to be best. The new missionaries desperately needed some experience, and once again the Abernathys were tapped as experienced missionaries to give help in getting the fledgling work underway.

"That means we're old," John kidded Jewell when the word "experienced" came up in the conference with Cauthen.

"I don't know, John," Jewell mused. "If you'd get some clothes, you might look pretty good."

She laughed heartily at the little joke. The fact was when they sailed for the Philippines that fall, they had few clothes beyond those on their backs. A Japanese-made suit and a couple of missionary hand-me-down dresses made up their wardrobe.

In Manila they were met by the new missionaries, for the most part still language students, and briefed on the contacts that had been made among the Chinese in the city. Soon John and Jewell were giving themselves unstintingly to beginning a witness in Manila and advising the young missionaries.

That proved to be a harder task than they anticipated. They were senior missionaries and had called the shots for a long time. The younger missionaries did not fall into that pattern with ease, and there were days of tension.

Soon they had a church started in Manila, and helped organize the new missionaries into the Philippine Baptist Mission. John tried to put his heart into the new work. He was grateful to be able to use the Chinese language again. He had been frustrated in Korea at that point. Jewell found all she could put her hand to with Bible classes among the women, home visitation, and opening her apartment to guests. It was very sparsely furnished, but she liked to share it.

Shortly after they arrived from Japan the Abernathys entertained Duke McCall, now president of Southern Baptist Theological Seminary, and W. A. Criswell, pastor of the prestigious First Baptist Church in Dallas, Texas. Criswell discovered that he and John wore the same size shoe, and when he realized John had only one pair of shoes, he gave John a pair of his.

"Now you'll have two pairs of shoes," he said exuberantly to John as he patted him on the back.

"How can I fill your shoes?" John asked, partly in jest, partly in awe at the famed preacher's graciousness.

In fact, Criswell was touched by the two missionaries who had learned that things have little meaning and who demonstrated the real values in life so beautifully.

Early in October John, out of breath, burst into their apartment. "Guess what, sweetheart!"

"My goodness, John, you'll have a heart attack that way. Okay, I give up. What?"

"The Ahns are safe in Pusan!" John's eyes were moist.

"Well, praise God!" Jewell said softly. The Ahns had been at the top of their prayer list.

John read the letter from Mrs. Ahn. They had made it to the safety of Pusan, leaving Seoul in John's car the very day the Abernathys flew out. Somehow, despite roadblocks and breakdowns, they stayed ahead of the Communist advance all the way to the Pusan perimeter.

John kept a sharp eye on events in Korea. In September, MacArthur engineered a brilliant counterattack highlighted by a dramatic amphibious landing at Inchon. It was hailed as one of the classic maneuvers in the history of war. This began a full-scale push to the 38th parallel.

John and Jewell followed the situation closely because John insisted God would enable them to go back to continue what they had started.

By November he felt sure they would be able to return to Seoul at an early date. MacArthur's forces had driven the North Koreans back beyond the 38th parallel. Then he continued the push all the way to the Yalu River, disregarding fears on the part of many that the Chinese Communists would retaliate.

In early October, when United Nations forces were approaching the Yalu, John wrote Ed Dozier in Japan, Baker Cauthen, and M. Theron Rankin suggesting that they meet soon in Seoul to begin a survey of both North and South Korea.

"One day now the great churches of the North will be free of Communist rule, and we will be able to preach in all of Korea. It's going to be a tremendous undertaking. We must plan now."

John also urged the Board to prepare for a massive relief program. His experience with relief to postwar days in Shantung convinced him that the need would be still greater in Korea.

Paul Caudill, chairman of the Baptist World Alliance's Relief Committee, wrote John asking him to help formulate needs.

On November 25, the Chinese struck suddenly. So-called volunteers from the Chinese army—the Chinese never admitted they were in the war as a nation—flooded across the Yalu River and ripped into the United Nations lines in human tidal waves. The annals of modern warfare had recorded nothing like it. The troops under MacArthur's command were soon fighting for their lives. Many were trapped in pockets, especially along the Sea of Japan, facing Dunkirk-like withdrawals. John's dreams for a witness in a united Korea were crushed.

On the last day of 1950, the second invasion of South Korea in less than a year began as advancing Chinese troops poured across the 38th parallel and moved on Seoul once more.

John and Jewell Abernathy in Manila mapped the events as they listened to their shortwave radio. Night after night John returned from his work to meet Jewell who carried on a similar work in another part of town. They had their meal, filled each other in on the day's events, and then listened to the armed services broadcast.

One night they heard that Dr. Bill Wallace, Southern Baptist missionary doctor in Wuchow, South China, had been arrested. Fear for his safety gripped both. They admired the young doctor. John had felt a sense of identification with him ever since he had carreid medical supplies over the Hump to him during Wallace's refugee hospital days in West China. A later report confirmed their fears. Wallace was dead.

The young doctor's martyrdom served to deepen John's hatred for communism. For him the world and Christendom were locked in a death struggle with this secular religion. Every brush he had with it was brutal, violent, and evil. In his prayers he asked God to help him love the people involved despite his feelings about their ideology.

John had hoped to be back in Seoul by the first of the year, but in January it was retaken by the Communists. He and Jewell wrote letters to try to find out what was happening to the Baptists in Korea. Little information was available. What news did come dismayed them.

Pastor Lee had been killed by the Communists.

Shortly after Seoul fell, a warrant was issued for Lee's arrest. By staying in church member's homes, he successfully avoided apprehension for some weeks. Then his wife sent word to him that she had papers only he could sign. He and Deacon Kim slipped into Lee's house under the cover of night, greeted his wife and family, and processed the papers. As they started to leave, the house was surrounded by Communists who had been tipped off as to his presence there. Lee and Kim were bound and carried off.

There was no trial, John learned. The two were taken to a river to be shot and dumped so that the tides would carry away the evidence.

The first place they were taken was not suitable because the tides were not operating as had been thought. The two men were left tied on the beach while their executioners looked for a better location. While they were alone, Pastor Lee helped Deacon Kim work free of his bonds.

Pastor Lee said, "I am old, but you are young. I am ready to be with my Master, but you have years of service left. Please go."

They heard the voices of their captors returning. Quickly embracing the old pastor, Deacon Kim fled. As he reached safety, he heard the shots which ushered Pastor Lee into the Lord's presence.

John and Jewell knew that many believers, both in China and in occupied Korea, were paying the ultimate price for their faith.

In February, United Nations troops recaptured Seoul and contained the Chinese advance not far from demarcation lines where the conflict had begun.

Shortly after the first of the year, John wrote to one of the top commanders under Douglas MacArthur in Korea, General Matthew Ridgeway, regarding a return to Korea at that time.

Before posting the letter, he said to Jewell, "I believe General Ridgeway will remember me from Shantung days. He is a fine man and straightforward, and I believe I can trust his answer. If he thinks it's all right to come back, I don't think we ought to delay any longer."

While waiting for a reply from Ridgeway, John responded to a request by Baker Cauthen to make a survey trip to the southern part of the Philippine Islands, specifically to Davao City on the island of Mindanao and to Cebu, the tiny island midway between Luzon and Mindanao.

John departed on March 9 for Davao, asking the Lord to open the way for him. As soon as he deplaned in Davao City, a friendly American introduced himself. The American, a Mr. Frazier, who had headed the Columbian Rope Company in the Philippines since 1916, was most thoughtful of John's welfare. After learning that he was representing the Foreign Mission Board to survey the possibilities of new work there, Mr. Frazier insisted that John accompany him to the city in his car. He secured a room for the missionary at the Davao Club and introduced him to several American and British businessmen.

That night John knelt and thanked a God who would order every step of a man's way. He definitely thought Mr. Frazier's appearance was an answer to prayer.

The next morning he made contact with Congregational missionaries and with Christian Missionary Alliance personnel. It was soon evident to him that no one working in the area had yet touched "the hem of the garment," as John wrote to Cauthen in his report.

After three days of discussing the situation with various Christian leaders, both Filipino and Chinese, John boarded a plane for Cebu.

The second largest city in the Philippine Islands, Cebu included a Chinese Christian congregation, with a pastor whom John had known in China. The two men met like long-lost brothers. John was shown the island and the small work that was there.

He found several Christians of Baptist background who claimed that if Southern Baptists came to Cebu, it would be an answer to prayer. With leadership, they would begin work immediately.

Returning to Manila, John typed out a full report to Dr. Cauthen, recommending that two couples be sent to Davao City and two to Cebu to begin work among the Filipinos and Chinese. He included details related to the logistics of getting couples in, arranging for living quarters, and a survey of the various language problems that would prevail.

He went to the post office to mail the letter and found there a letter that was unmistakably military. It was from General Ridgeway. A smile broke on John's face as he read, "I see no reason why you shouldn't return to Pusan in the near future. I suggest you make application at the U.S. Embassy here at SACAP for clearance."

John broke the news gently to Jewell, however. Ridgeway was

careful to point out that women were not yet allowed to return unless they were nurses. But John need not have worried. Jewell rejoiced with him and assured him that the minute the Lord was through with her in Manila, he would provide the way for her to join him in Pusan.

Early in March 1951, John recieved word that he was to proceed directly to Tokyo for clearance into Korea. He could be processed through military headquarters there to enter Pusan if David Ahn would vouch for him and provide a place for him to live. The door was open.

Preparing to board the plane that would take him to Japan, John embraced Jewell at the Manila airport.

"Don't worry, Jewell. No separations like the last ones! I'll convince those fellows that you are a remarkable woman, and we'll clear you into Korea right soon."

She smiled, her eyes full and glistening, her glasses in her hand. "Do, John. Do tell them I must come."

John smiled at her. "I'll tell them what an extraordinary woman you are, how brave you are, how . . ."

She cut him short. "While you're talking to them, I'll be talking to the Lord."

Again they embraced. John waved, pulled the brim of his straw hat onto his forehead (he was in the habit of pushing it back until it perched on the rear of his head, and pulling it forward seemed to indicate he meant business), and boarded the plane.

Several hours later he was in Tokyo. He thought he would be there only a few hours. As it turned out, he was there three weeks before he could cut the red tape into Korea. Meanwhile, he received nothing but discouragement to his hope that Jewell could follow him.

"It's too uncertain," the military clerk with whom he had pled his case, replied. "This thing in Korea swings up and down so rapidly we never know where it's going to be next."

Then John's clearance came, and he boarded the military flight across the Tsushima Strait to Pusan.

As he debarked, he could see his friends, the Ahns. They were beautiful—thinner—but beautiful. They embraced John. Despite his protestations that he was too old for such things, he had to wipe tears from his cheeks. The three of them laughed and all tried to talk at once. Their hardships since parting only made the reunion sweeter.

Mr. Ahn claimed John's bags and led him to the parking lot where John's Ford stood, battered and worn, but operable.

John laid his hand on the hood, "You know, I never thought I'd see this thing again."

Ahn said quietly, "If you had not left it, you never would have seen us again."

John slipped an arm around Ahn's shoulder and gave him a brotherly hug. "I guess the Lord controls the logistics on things like this."

On the first Sunday after arriving in Pusan, the David Ahns proudly led John to the Baptist church where a large crowd of Korean Baptists gathered, most of them refugees from both north and south of the 38th parallel.

Just before the service John asked one of them about a mutual friend whom he had met during his first week in Korea. "I'm sorry," his informant said, "they took him away and we have never heard from him."

To inquiries about others he knew, he all too often got the response, "He is dead" or "She is dead."

Frantically, John looked at Ahn, who was interpreting for him. Ahn simply shook his head. "Many are gone."

As John stood up to speak, he noticed that many of them were pale and their clothes badly worn. It was obvious that many of them had suffered greatly since he last saw them.

After the service, John learned that some churches had been destroyed. Many members had lost their homes and farms. He knew their story was all too typical. Relief was needed in the area, not just among Baptists, but among hundreds of thousands of refugees streaming into Pusan. The $10,000 sent by Southern Baptists through the Foreign Mission Board for relief work seemed hopelessly inadequate.

First, John arranged to get new tires and badly needed repair for his car. Then he and David Ahn made a trip through war-torn sections of the liberated south to survey the situation. Just before leaving, he wrote Rankin, "I am missing Jewell like a front tooth and wish she were here, but Ambassador Muccio told me Monday there would be no women coming into Korea any time soon."

He added: "Our cable address is KOBAP. The name is established already. Let's pray KOBAP can made a difference here."

Jewell Abernathy became a persistent intercessor with God for her husband during the weeks that followed. But her intercession had to be drawn from time increasingly occupied with growing work among the Chinese in Manila.

She also discovered a new ministry—writing. In May 1951, a lengthy article in the Foreign Mission Board's magazine, *The Commission,* told the story of the new work in the Philippines. It had been a labor of love for Jewell, and an affirmation of a ministry to supporters back home that she felt was as important in the Lord's scheme of things as her ministry in the Philippines. John and Jewell had become convinced on each of their furloughs—during which they had worked very diligently and spread themsevles very thin—that missions was only as strong as the convictions and awareness of the people back home.

"Unless the people back home get behind the work abroad with prayer and with their lives, as well as with their gifts, then it will not go forward," Jewel wrote the magazine's editor.

When she posted the article to the editor of *The Commission,* she breathed a prayer that God would use it for just that.

Meanwhile, John's Davao City and Cebu survey report to Baker Cauthen was bearing fruit. Two couples were soon to arrive in the Philippines to begin work in Davao City.

To Jewell's surprise, letters from John came often. That he missed her was obvious with every letter. Missing him was as much a part of her life as breath itself.

"I'm afraid I've been discouraged about your coming," he wrote. "I told them that you were a woman with great experience in difficult situations and able to cope with almost anything. In fact, I may have poured it on too thick. I'm not sure they believed me. But you are that kind of woman."

They had been married over twenty-five years and had shared thirty years of service as missionaries.

"Lord, where do the years go?" she asked aloud after reading his letter.

Then memories flooded consciousness: of Shantung, of revival, the war, separation, of faces with whom they had lived and ministered and shared great difficulties as well as the Lord's blessings. Yes, the flight of years was possible.

John Abernathy worked hard. He nursed his Ford along from place to place across the scarred landscape, dispensing relief items to the pitiful human debris left in the wake of the war that had swept back and forth over the countryside like the scythe of a grim reaper.

The country people had been ready to harvest their crops when the Chinese swept down from the north. They had abandoned all and fled before the Red terror, though it did not take long for the United Nations troops to drive them back north again. When the farmers returned home, their crops were ruined. Starvation was an ever-present threat.

Early one evening John and David Ahn, permanently employed by John as advisor and interpreter, pulled into the little community of Chilsen, where the Seven Hills Church which John had visited earlier in his ministry was located. It was there that he had seen remarkable evidence of obedience in tithes of every sort, and the building that had been begun with great sacrifice, though it had not been completed.

They weren't sure what they would find, but Baptist friends began to appear from everywhere to greet them like long-lost relatives. John and David discovered that the Chilsen church and community were caught up in an exciting revival that was transforming lives and yielding miracles of all sorts in their midst. Even more dramatic was the story behind the revival.

Children from the village had been playing on the beach of the Cum River, which runs through the town. During the night a mine had been washed up on shore, and the children went to inspect the strange piece of metal. It exploded, and forty-one of the children were killed immediately. Many others were severely wounded.

Some of the children who were killed came from the homes of the Baptist church members at Seven Hills. They included the pastor's son. A deacon lost two sons. There were nights of deep grief and soul-searching. One by one the Christian parents involved began to see in the tragedy what they thought was the Lord's hand. Their response was to complete the church with great sacrifice. The example of their sacrifice in the midst of grief astounded so many people that the witness of the church suddenly had new power.

When Ahn and Abernathy drove away from Chilsen two days later, they were moved beyond understanding at what they had seen of the dedication of the people in Chilsen. John called it "the church of great price."

After leaving Chilsen, Abernathy and his companion started for a place called Wontang where the decimated Korean Baptists planned to hold their annual convention. They were unable to traverse the heavily damaged roads with their car. With his remarkable ability to convince others and to talk to anybody of any station in life, John talked a GI into giving them a ride on a hospital train bound for Taejon. Unfortunately, the hospital train was late, but an ammunition train came by. Soon John Abernathy and David Ahn were rumbling across the Korean countryside propped up against ammunition boxes and sharing C-rations with two GIs who seemed delighted with their companionship. The GIs had the engineer make a special stop for John and David.

The most solemn part of the convention was a memorial service for sixty-one Baptists, including four pastors, who had been killed by the Communists since the last convention.

A ride on a northbound hospital train returned John and Ahn to their car and the work in Pusan.

After returning from the trip, John wrote Cauthen that he thought their main emphasis for the present should be centered at Pusan. The only area that had been consistently safe, it was the refugee center. John urged Cauthen to send one of the missionary doctors formerly in China, perhaps N. A. Bryan, to develop a clinic.

"These people have no place to turn for medical aid," he wrote.

He also reported taking an option on a building that looked reasonable in price and suitable for a multiple ministry.

Cauthen wrote back that not only would Dr. Bryan be coming, but Rex Ray also. Ray, who had served with Bill Wallace in South China, was, like John, a veteran. John looked forward to his coming. Cauthen also sent a check to close the deal on the building.

"Southern Baptists are responding with open hearts to the needs there," Cauthen wrote.

Soon John, the Korean Baptists, and several American soldiers who were Baptists were busy renovating the building. They set up living quarters for the missionaries and Korean workers, an area for church services, and a clinic.

In July the bells began to ring with news that a cease-fire had been signed. Truce talks began at a place called Panmunjom. This meant an end to the suffering and new hope for the millions south of the 38th parallel. For John, it signaled the possibility that Jewell would be able to join him.

The Baptists celebrated with a baptismal service in the ocean near Pusan.

John waded into the waters late in the afternoon as the sun began to settle over the surrounding hills. Several hundred Korean Baptists sang on the shore. John turned to greet the candidates who waded out to him. David and Soon Do Ahn's eldest son, Solomon, was among them. John's two colleagues, David and Soon Do, beamed through their tears as they sang with the others on the shore.

As he placed each of the new converts beneath the waters in baptism and raised them, symbolizing their new life in Christ, he felt a deep sense of well-being because of what God was allowing him to do. That night as he climbed wearily into his bed, he thought of all that was still to be done. But Dr. Bryan and Rex Ray would soon be there. Additional money had been made available. Together, they could do much more than he could do alone.

"God, give me the strength," he said before falling into an exhausted sleep.

The next week John was thrust into an ironic kind of ministry. He was given permission to preach at the Chinese POW camp. As he prepared his heart in prayer for the assignment, it occurred to him that though he could no longer go to China, China was coming to him.

The first group of prisoners to whom he preached were wounded. His heart went out to them. Many were horribly burned. Some were crippled for life. John was introduced by several American officers, using Korean interpreters. When he stood up and began to speak in clear Mandarin, the prisoners cheered him. They were glad to hear their own language. Their response astounded John and the officials who cleared him.

There were also some setbacks. In mid-summer John returned to his room to find it empty of everything that wasn't nailed down.

A robber had visited him. Once again John was reduced to what he had on his back. However, he had enough money to buy a few necessities and very little time to worry about his loss. Somebody else did, though. A few days later he recieved from one of the U.S. Navy ships in Pusan several boxes full of khaki clothes just his size.

"The Lord does provide," John said, trying on his new clothes.

Early in the fall renovation of the building was finished. No little part of the accomplishment was due to the help of eager Baptist servicemen.

In October, John wrote Baker Cauthen that he had received several tents to put up on adjacent property and that one day an army major had left twenty-five sacks of cement and the next day all the electrical supplies they were going to need. Three days later three truckloads of lumber showed up. After that, paint and five hospital beds with accompanying mattresses arrived. John confided to David Ahn that he was scared to inquire where these things were coming from.

Sometimes at the invitation of Baptist chaplains, he traveled on troop trains to staging camps near the front lines. On one occasion, after preaching to front line troops and then to a M.A.S.H. unit nearby, he returned on the hospital train with those wounded in the last days before the truce. He stopped at every bed for a visit with each GI. Often at their request, he had prayer with them.

There were some lonely moments. John would go to his little corner in the "Baptist Building" to grab some much-needed sleep and, lying on his cot, wonder if Jewell would ever get there. He had learned that four American Methodist missionary women were in Pusan and hoped this meant Jewell could come.

In late November, John received word that Jewell's efforts to come to Korea were again blocked. Even a visit permit was turned down. When Cauthen learned of their disappointment, he suggested that John arrange to visit Jewell in the Philippines as soon as he could get clear.

John didn't get Jewell for Christmas, but he got Dr. Bryan and Rex Ray. He didn't realize how thin he had spread himself until they got there to help pick up the load.

Christmas parties were numerous and joyous. GIs joined in. They took great delight in showing up with supplies for dinner and presents for orphans in the area.

"Where did you get these things?" John asked one of them in wonder.

"We got them through midnight requisitions, padre."

"Midnight requisitions?"

"Yes, it's a technical term used in the military."

Walking through Korean cold that night, bundled against the chill, the three men—Bryan, Abernathy, and Ray—talked of the Lord's leadership in their lives. They agreed it was a mystery how God ordered their comings and goings. They talked also about plans for a hospital. Could they name it after Bill Wallace, the doctor who was martyred in South China? Rex had worked with him and thought it a good idea.

As they walked it was obvious they were in a Buddhist country. Many signs and symbols around them attested to the fact. But from time to time the soft sounds of a Christmas hymn wafted its way down the street, increasing their nostalgia and warming their hearts.

At the Korean Baptist Church more than five hundred people were present. They sounded a note of hope for the future.

John said to the Ahns, "Hope may be as important as food and clothing."

They nodded in agreement.

John and his colleagues celebrated the New Year by starting a clinic. Dr. Bryan was immediately inundated with patients. John and Rex continued to go to POW camps to preach. Since Rex was Cantonese-speaking and John was Mandarin-speaking, they were able to reach the majority of the prisoners in their own language.

In mid-January John was told that Jewell had been granted clearance to come to Korea. He wrote her a long detailed letter, telling what she should bring, and informed her he had already lined up work for her at the coming Baptist convention.

"When you get here," he wrote, "we'll organize the Korean Baptist Mission."

But as the weeks dragged by and her papers did not come, severe disappointment set in. Only their faith in the Lord's leadership sustained them. Jewell continued to encounter people who needed her in Manila. In fact, each week brought a new situation to help her understand why she was still there.

As for John, his incredibly busy schedule helped offset the loneliness he felt without his mate.

Rex Ray wrote Baker Cauthen, "John drives around like Jehu, doing more than any one man ought to do."

In May Cauthen insisted that John return to Manila for a visit with Jewell.

"If Jewell can't get to John, let's get John to Jewell," he wrote.

"We're a little old for a third honeymoon," Jewell suggested to John as he got off the plane in Manila.

"Who says so?" John replied.

For three weeks they had that honeymoon. The time passed impossibly fast. Then John had to go back to Korea. He had been asked to represent the Mission at inauguration ceremonies in Seoul for President-elect Syngman Rhee. With the inauguration invitation came an invitation also to attend a reception at the Korean White House.

Back in Pusan, John laid aside the clothes that bore the daily marks of refugee work, the dust of prisoner-of-war camps, the snags and lint and smell of work in the midst of impoverished humanity. He donned a new suit for the great occasion, caught the United Nations express on Thursday night, and arrived in Seoul early the morning of the inauguration. Sleepy as he was, he was caught up in the excitement.

Rhee was a staunch anti-Communist and a firm believer in the future of his land. He had paid a great price for his nationalism under the Japanese. His hands bore the marks of imprisonment and torture. John was struck by his snow-white hair and strong eyes. Th new president's age, nearing eighty years, earned his respect and power in a culture which honored its elders.

John was greeted by President and Mrs. Rhee and Vice President Hahn, and enjoyed additional conversation with them at the reception. He was also introduced to the American Army Chief Mark Clark and his wife. All seemed to know about John's work and the contribution he, Dr. Bryan, and Rex Ray were making in Pusan. President Rhee took time to thank John and urged him to call again.

That night John took the United Nations train back to Pusan—another all-night ride after the wearying, but exciting day. It seemed hard to realize that he had been in the midst of the pomp and circumstance on which the eyes of the world had focused that day.

No use letting that kind of thing go to his head, he thought as he put his head back to grab a few hours of sleep. There was much to be done the next day. If Jewell could just come . . .

A month later Jewell did come. Seen off at the airport by the many Chinese students with whom she worked and missionaries who had grown to love her and to regard her as a mother in their midst, she boarded the Northwest Airline plane for Tokyo and then Pusan.

John, along with twenty-five Korean Baptists and a mountain of flowers, met the plane. Tears flowed freely.

Jewell was so excited she could hardly contain herself. Even the drab rooms they shared with Dr. Bryan, Rex Ray, and the David Ahns and their children did not undermine her excitement.

Her high spirits lasted nearly a week, the time crammed with welcomes and gifts. The first part of the next week John missed her and went looking for her. She was in their room.

"What are you doing here? Are you sick?"

"No," she said, "I'm just having a hard time living and prospering in the confusion you people think is normal."

John laughed heartily, "You'll get used to it."

9
Such a Brief Time

The war in Korea refused to come to a clear-cut end. Talks at Panmunjom seemed to stumble on and on with major problems developing over minor matters. A key concern related to prisoner exchange. The United States protested over the way prisoners were being treated. Stories of psychological torture called brainwashing and reports of death of prisoners in Communist hands were maddening and depressing.

In November of 1952 Dwight D. Eisenhower was elected President of the United States. One of his platform promises was that he would terminate the Korean hostilities as soon as possible, and in December he went to Korea as he promised. John and Jewell and the force of missionaries now increased by Ruby Wheat and Irene Branum and a few months later Lucy Wright, missionary nurses from China, took heart.

In the spring of 1953, however, another breakdown in negotiations occurred, and the Communists launched new attacks all along the front. This time the United Nations forces held and the Chinese suffered an estimated seventy thousand casualties in the effort.

Syngman Rhee was reluctant to sign an armistice that would divide Korea. As much as John longed for peace, as much as he hated war with its tragic refugees and lines of displaced people and hordes of starved children, he tended to agree with President Rhee.

"What kind of nation would this be with a million Chinese Communists looking down their throats?" he asked Jewell.

He noted smugly that nearly fifteen thousand Chinese prisoners refused to go back on the Communist side and were sent instead to Formosa. Many of them had trusted Christ under John's preaching, and he knew they wanted no part of communism.

"How many more like them must there be in China!" he said to Jewell.

But in July 1953, the armistice was signed, and the battle lines became the boundary between North and South Korea.

Left only was the task for the historians—to total the carnage and ponder the meaning. An estimated thirty-three thousand Americans were killed along with five thousand other United Nations personnel. Over seventy thousand South Korean soldiers perished. Over two hundred and sixty thousand of these three groups were wounded. Another hundred thousand suffered unbelievable horrors in Chinese prison camps.

Communist casualties totaled an estimated 1,600,000, nearly 60 percent of them Chinese. In addition, the Communists suffered an estimated four hundred thousand nonbattle deaths from disease.

A more staggering figure was the estimated 3,500,000 North and South Korean civilians who died from causes directly attributable to the war.

The necessity of continued American troop presence in Korea despite the cessation of formal hostilities opened remarkable opportunity which John and his colleagues bought up eagerly.

American soldiers and equipment and materials turned to rebuilding the country. John directed ground-clearing for church buildings and assumed supervision of schools, children's homes, and homes started by American soldiers to care for the displaced, the refugees, and orphans.

The Korean Baptist Mission was organized with John formally elected its executive secretary-treasurer In 1954 the first missionaries appointed for Korea, the Ted Dowells, joined the "old China hands," and the work grew rapidly.

New churches were organized and church buildings rebuilt. Displaced congregations regathered and reported waves of revival.

Faced with a sea of misery, the clinic continued to expand and plans for a hospital were pushed. More missionary doctors were requested from the Foreign Mission Board.

A seminary was organized in Taejon. Through it all, John, as Rex Ray said, "drove like Jehu."

Though busy with relief administration, John could not resist opportunities to preach. One weekend he went with a rural pastor to visit his congregation. They drove as far as they could and then began to walk. John asked the pastor, who was strolling leisurely ahead of him, how far it was.

"Just a little way," the pastor replied.

On they plodded, following the meanderings of a sparkling stream that ran down a hillside. Below and above them people were transplanting young rice sprouts in precariously carved fields. At various points they could see a half dozen villages with straw-thatched houses.

As they drew near one, John said, "This must be it."

But they kept walking.

Finally, they came to a small village and walked right through it. John feared they were in for still another mile when they met a group of men in the white traditional Korean dress. The men greeted them and took them to a small room on the edge of the village.

John's interpreter indicated they were to be refreshed before going to the church. John slipped off his shoes and sat on the floor to eat the boiled eggs and drink the barley tea set before him. The walk had left him with a ravenous appetite. It was all he could do to eat ceremoniously, as was proper for the occasion, rather than voraciously, the way he felt.

Then the leaders indicated that it was time to go the church, and they walked across the village to one of the most beautiful churches John had ever seen. It was a huge tree with wide spreading branches under whose shade sat such a host of people that he could not count them. He estimated three hundred people there, sitting on mats to await his coming. They began to sing as the leaders arrived. With great ceremony, they took a chair to the front and sat John before the multitude while the singing continued.

John tilted his head back and looked up into the vast canopy of the tree above him and then down at the smiling crowd singing God's praises. He decided there was no adequate way to record his feelings.

Just before Christmas Dr. Bryan flew to Japan to visit with medical personnel in Fukuoka who were supplying help and equipment. When he returned to Pusan, John met him. As they started back to the city from the airfield the car began to veer right and left. John spun the wheel helplessly. Dr. Bryan grabbed for support, aware that they were out of control.

"The steering column is broken," John shouted. "Hold on!"

The car turned sharply left, almost turning over, then plunged from an eight-foot bank into an irrigation ditch. The water rose rapidly but stopped while their heads were still above it. John extricated himself immediately, but Dr. Bryan was having difficulty. Wading around to the other side, John wedged the door open and began to pull the doctor out through the mud. As he did, Bryan yelped with pain. Both identified what was wrong. Dr. Bryan's arm was broken halfway between the shoulder and the elbow. As they climbed to the road, dripping and covered with mud, an army jeep pulled up and soldiers jumped out to help them.

"Don't worry, John," Dr. Bryan said. "Let's just praise God that we weren't killed."

As they bumped along in the jeep toward the Swedish hospital, John tried to comfort Dr. Bryan. "You know, I was just thinking of all those places up-country where that could have happened. You know, where the cliffs are a thousand feet."

"Some sense of humor!" Dr. Bryan grimaced.

After Jewell's return and as the missionary force in Korea grew, the Abernathys enjoyed telling the newcomers about their early days there. John, Rex Ray, and N. A. Bryan, who had been eating Korean food army-style, were immediately captivated by Jewell's cooking. First one, then another, and finally all three would come dragging in: John from days of wading through red tape, going from one prisoner-of-war camp to another, and working with a dozen children's homes; Rex Ray from the countryside where he was distributing relief and contacting churches in need; and Dr. Bryan from seeing over three hundred patients. As a man, they would look up from the meal at the smiling Jewell and say, "How did we ever get along without you?"

Jewell smiled, "Why is it that the hard days are often the best?"

There was too much ahead of them, however, to get caught up in too much looking behind.

About the time the armistice was signed, the David Ahns boarded a plane in Pusan for Fort Worth, Texas. They were to spend some time in seminary there and in traveling throughout the United States sharing the story of Korean Baptists. The Abernathys felt as if they were losing both arms.

Also, bound for the States was a young Korean lad named Timothy

Cho who had become like a son to John and Jewell. They had high hopes that he would return to Korea someday and be a part of the new leadership that would take over in the days ahead.

Shortly after the Ahns left, John bought a house in Seoul on behalf of the Mission to be the Mission headquarters. He prepared an apartment in it for Jewell and himself and they moved there from Pusan. They were invited almost immediately to visit President and Mrs. Rhee. John was delighted to introduce them to his Jewell, and the couples visited at length.

As they left, Jewell said, "John, I don't know about you. Everywhere you go you seem to get tied in with kings and presidents, and princes and generals."

One of the first persons he had introduced Jewell to in Pusan had been the dowager queen of Korea and two of the young princesses. Korea had been a kingdom prior to the Japanese occupation and, though now a republic, the royal family was still accorded much respect and honor.

John laughed. It was a wonder to him also.

"Who ever would have thought it of a country boy?" he said. "God leads people in strange ways."

That same summer they suffered a devastating blow with word that M. Theron Rankin had died in Richmond. The executive secretary had been a personal friend, a fellow missionary for twenty years, and then their area secretary. The hurt was deep. John recalled their days on the *Gripsholm* together when they returned from Japanese war camps.

"He was a man of great faith and vision," he said to Jewell.

They were encouraged with word that their friend and area secretary, Baker Cauthen, was to become the new executive secretary of the Foreign Mission Board.

"There's not a finer man for the task," John assured Jewell.

"You don't have to tell me that," she said. "I write him as many letters as you do."

John laughed. Jewell was the most prolific letter writer he had ever known.

After Cauthen's election, news came that Winston Crawley was to be their new area secretary. Winston and his wife Margaret had been with them in the Philippines. As Chinese-language students, the Crawleys had been displaced from Peiping when the Communist advance began. The two of them helped found the seminary and the Philippine Mission in Baguio.

In 1954 Jewell received a cable with news that her father had suffered a stroke. A letter that followed said he had rallied for a time but seemed to be going downhill. They had not planned to go on furlough until 1956, but Crawley asked them to go in 1955 as soon as the buildings in Pusan and Taejon were complete.

"Whether he will be alive when I get home is not sure," Jewell wrote Crawley.

A few weeks later word came that he had died. She knew then she would have to wait until she got to heaven to see him again.

She remembered the closeness they shared after her mother died and she had taken over the care of her brothers and sisters. Tears flowed copiously as she thought of their tender leave-taking on the train in Kansas City in 1920. She remember his sitting quietly on the porch during John's imprisonment, listening to her play the accordion and encouraging her when she was blue.

In 1955 the David Ahns returned to Korea. It should have been a glorious day for the Abernathys for whom the Ahns had been such a great joy and comfort in their early days in Korea. Their sense of camaraderie, their willingness to share suffering and deprivation, their courage and faith had been of indescribable comfort to the missionaries. But something had happened while the Ahns were in the States.

They had gone under the sponsorship of the Korean Mission for a stated length of time. When the time was up, there was still a great demand for them in the churches, and they enjoyed the United States so much that they were reluctant to leave. When the Mission put pressure on them to return to Korea, they were hurt.

Upon their return, John and Jewell greeted them, but sensed a coolness. A few weeks later as John traveled with Ahn to Taejon and the seminary, which John served not only as trustee but also as founder and first president, John got the distinct impression that Ahn was hoping he would resign in favor of himself. John felt the trustees would be unwilling to turn to Ahn. But he could not tell David that and so the gulf widened.

More damaging to their relationship was a misunderstanding over the house in which the Ahns lived and which they shared with the Abernathys in the early days. The house had been a gift to Mrs. Ahn from the royal family of Korea for favors she rendered them.

During the time the Ahns were in the United States, the Korean government—now a republic—announced that it was going to sell at auction all property that formerly belonged to the royal family. John wrote the Ahns immediately to see what they wanted to do. Other Korean Baptists counseled John to try to purchase the property for the Mission. The Ahns wrote back and said they would like to buy it personally but had no money. John then purchased it for the Mission. When the Ahns returned, they moved into the house, and though they were unable to make the down payment, insisted that the Mission transfer the property to them.

John's sense of commitment to straightforward business principles while serving as the Mission's treasurer, would not give way to his friendship. He pointed out to the Ahns that he could not transfer the property to them without the down payment.

The gulf widened and brought deep heartbreak for John and Jewell Abernathy. David Ahn began publishing a paper called "Baptist Press" for the Korean convention and ran an issue on the history of Baptist work before and after it was called Baptist. Despite John's deep involvement, there was no mention of his name.

In 1955 John filed a report for Paul Caudill of the Baptist World Alliance Relief Committee for the London meeting of the Alliance. In it he reported that he had channeled over a quarter million dollars of Baptist relief funds to needy persons and groups throughout Korea during the five years he represented this cause. Recorded simply as the cold statistics of an audit, it was nevertheless a remarkable story of heroism, heartbreak, and long hours of work.

John and Jewell boarded the plane for their furlough in December, 1955. The toll taken by their years in Korea had been high. John would soon celebrate his sixtieth birthday, and they both knew they needed time away from Mission responsibilities. Perhaps in the States they could lose their heartbreak over the strain with the Ahns. Perhaps they could gain some perspective in dealing with a growing Mission which no longer saw eye to eye with them on every matter or automatically deferred to their seniority.

They were proud of the Mission. Strong young couples were giving remarkably mature service. The older China hands who began the work were moving off the scene. Dr. Bryan had not returned from furlough; the Rex Rays and the Earl Parkers, along with Ruby Wheat, Irene Branum, and Lucy Wright were still there, but getting along in years.

People like the Ted Dowells, the Robert Wrights, the Dan Rays, the Parkes Marlers, the J. G. Goodwins, and the Don Joneses were picking up the leadership and providing the energy for expansion.

But there were still clouds on the horizon. The Ahns formed a faction with others who were dissatisfied with the Mission's policies, and a hint of tension was in the air.

John and Jewell boarded a Korean flight to Tokyo, and then changed onto a Pan American flight nonstop to San Francisco. John laid his head back on the seat to get some rest and begin the recovery of mind and body.

"Can you imagine how many days and nights we have spent crossing this ocean," Jewell commented. "Now we're going to do it in an afternoon and a night."

She leaned back also, looking out the window, shaking her head with the wonder of it all. John took off his glasses and rubbed each eye wearily. Where did his wife get all that energy and constant excitement? Thank the Lord they shared it most of the time. It had been one of the joys of their married life.

The next morning they were in San Francisco, ooing and aahing over the vistas as if they had never traveled before. Dr. Harold Graves, president of Golden Gate Baptist Theological Seminary, met them and took them directly to the seminary for rest and a chapel engagement. Visiting with students in the beautiful bay city and speaking in chapel gave them a chance to ease back into the culture. It was good to be home.

They took delivery of a new Chevrolet that John had arranged to have awaiting them, and began a drive across the United States— something they had always wanted and never been able to do. They spent Christmas in Winston-Salem with John's relatives, the first Christmas John had spent with his family since he had left the States thirty-five years before.

Then they moved to Tulsa, where they arranged to spend their furlough close to some of Jewell's relatives. The spring was a busy but delightful time. John and Jewell were in demand in Woman's Missionary Union conventions and churches throughout the country.

In April John was invited to Richmond to address the Foreign Mission Board and to confer with Baker Cauthen and Winston Crawley and members of the Committee on the Orient.

He was always introduced as Dr. Abernathy and was a little embarrassed when a press representative asked him where he received his doctorate. John had secured the degree through a correspondence course with an Indiana institution. He had not used it much except in Oriental government circles where it seemed to open doors when nothing else would.

In the summer, both spoke at Ridgecrest and had a chance for fellowship with four Korean students they had helped to send to the States to attend various colleges and seminaries. They were overjoyed with the progress of Timothy Cho, who was making an outstanding academic record at Southern Baptist Theological Seminary at Louisville, Kentucky. The young Korean was like a son to them.

Early in the summer they were surprised when the David Ahns appeared in Tulsa. The Ahns had returned to the States to confer with Baptist World Alliance officials and came to visit the Abernathys. The four prayed together and talked of reconciliation and love. Nevertheless, after the Ahns departed John retained an uneasy feeling. Somehow he continued to feel that the matters between them had not been resolved. Letters a few months later from Korea confirmed his fears, and once again the sense of failure that so often haunted him when he thought of the situation hovered in the background. He knew it represented more than just a breakdown in a personal relationship. It also represented a rift between many of those with whom John had begun the work and the Baptist Mission.

John and Jewell's trip back to Korea in December 1956, took an unusual turn. They booked passage on the USS *President Cleveland* and were delighted to find that two new missionary couples en route to the Orient, the Troy Bennets to Pakistan and the Ernest Glasses to Singapore, were to be their companions. After they put their luggage in their modest cabins, the captain and purser came to John and said he was to have a different cabin. Soon John and Jewell were standing in the midst of the most luxurious cabin they had ever seen, and the captain was explaining to John that he would serve as the ship's chaplain. John enjoyed the opportunity and made the cabin available to the new missionary couples and their children. He was even more surprised to find out in a letter from Baker Cauthen a few weeks later that the shipping line had refunded the price of his ticket.

"What d'ya know, I finally paid my way," John said when the word came.

On the voyage John and Jewell talked together of their future. The term of service in Korea had been adjusted to four years by the Foreign Mission Board. This meant they would be eligible in 1960 to return home.

"Do you realize, Jewell," John asked, "that if we go home in '60, I'll be sixty-five when it comes time to return to Korea?"

Jewell was quiet. She was two years older than John and more aware of the passage of time than he.

"Now, the Board will allow us to serve until I'm seventy, on a year-to-year basis. And perhaps the Mission needs us. I don't know. I've been everything out here—treasurer, president of the seminary, liaison with the government, but now there are younger men. I really need to resign my position at the seminary—living up in Seoul as we do and my trying to commute—and there are any number of good men who can move into the treasurer's position."

Still Jewell was silent. When John talked like this she never interrupted his thinking.

"I think if we knew the language, Jewell—if we weren't a couple of Mandarin-speaking China hands in a Korean-speaking country—it would be worth it. But as it is, I think it's going to be time for us to wind things up, come home while we still have some strength and vigor to go into the churches and contact the young people and press home the missionary claims."

John stopped and looked at Jewell.

She responded, "I think you're right, John. I think this is it. Let's go back and give it our best and wind it up right."

John looked preoccupied as he walked to the stateroom window and gazed out over the broad expanse of the Pacific.

"Yes, let's try to wind it up right. Let's pray to God that somehow some of the problems will be solved by then."

They returned to a joyous round of celebrations. John and Jewell came to realize that in Korea a man's sixty-first birthday was a very special event. It was the beginning of the second major portion of his life, according to the Koreans.

"An optimistic thought," commented John.

They feted him throughout South Korea for days after the actual birthday had come and gone. It gave him a chance to renew fellowship and touch base with pastors and congregations that the press of business had kept him from too long.

In 1957 a spiritual awakening came in the Mission. It wasn't exactly a Shantung revival, but each missionary went through a soul-searching experience and the result was a sweet fellowship of sharing, confession, and forgiveness. Korean leaders, aware of what happened, were profoundly impressed. But that did not solve the Abernathys' number-one heartache. They were as estranged from the Ahns as ever.

The atmosphere gave John an opportunity to do something he had been wanting to do and that was to resign as president of the seminary. He had done it once before. This time they accepted and elected young Ted Dowell as the new president.

The trustees met during late March while it was still very cold. Korean winters can be bitingly cold, and a heavy snow fell during the meeting. John's hands and feet never seemed to warm up during the wintertime.

When he got home, he and Jewell prepared to go to bed.

He said, "Put on an extra blanket, Jewell; I never get warm anymore."

Jewell did, and got ready to listen to his report of the meeting. He told her of his good feeling about the seminary and his plans to go back for the dedication of the building and speak on Founder's Day.

Then he said, "Pretty soon we'll be at retirement age. The first thing we're going to do is go to Florida and find us a good home in the sun."

"Why Florida?" she asked.

"I've always wanted to go to Florida. And beside, I might get warm there."

The next year David Ahn was elected president of the convention, which turned out to be far from the healing event John had hoped. He tried hard to work with the man who had once been so close.

Mrs. Ahn was in the United States part of the time and her mother, one of the finest Korean Christians John had ever known, became ill and died before Mrs. Ahn could get back. John tried to minister to the family, but when Mrs. Ahn returned he realized that too much still stood between them. The matter of the house had been resolved, but the feelings had not.

Then it was 1959, and their last year. The Mission voted for Don Jones to take over the treasurer's work, and he moved to Seoul to begin working alongside John.

It seemed as if the whole year were one long goodbye party. John and Jewell made up their minds to enjoy it.

When they visited Taejon for the dedication of the Korean Baptist Theological Seminary, they were surprised to see a stone at the entrance bearing the Korean inscription: "In Honor of Dr. John Abernathy, A Servant of the Lord in the Orient for Forty Years. Founder, Trustee, and First President of the Korean Baptist Theological Seminary."

One of the Korean leaders spoke a tribute to Jewell, commending her for standing by her husband's side through such difficult years and with such a victorious spirit. Then he asked her if she would like to make a reply.

She smiled and said, "Whenever he is honored, I am honored."

There were gifts and tears and embraces. Through the years the Abernathys had become grandfather and grandmother to all the missionary children, and an increasing number of them crowded around John and Jewell during any Mission event.

The last official letter John opened was from Baker James Cauthen. He reviewed the work John and Jewell had done. As they read the letter, it was hard for them to realize there had only been thirty-five small Baptist churches when they arrived in Korea nine years before. Now there were over two hundred. They had been the only missionaries in the beginning. There were now thirty-five. And there were seven orphan homes, a seminary, and the Wallace Memorial Hospital.

But John knew that was not the whole story.

A major split had developed in Korean Baptist life that year, and though it had been on the horizon for some time, it had deeply grieved him. He prayed for reconciliation among the brethren.

Cauthen's letter continued, "You will be able to leave the field with the feeling of a job well done. It is seldom that a person is able to go into a field of work and see so much accomplished in such a brief time. . . ."

"Such a brief time." The phrase was apt for the way John felt.

As their plane gained altitude from Seoul, he looked out across the land, cold and dark with winter. But he knew the land would be green and promising come spring.

And off to the west across the Yellow Sea, a little farther than he could see, was Shantung. The names and faces of those with whom he had lived and shared his ministry began to parade across his mind.

"Such a brief time!"

John looked at Jewell and realized that she knew every thought in his head. He gripped her hand and both leaned back and let the great plane carry them home.

It doesn't take long to spend forty years in the Lord's service.

Epilogue

John and Jewell Abernathy did not retire in Florida as they had planned, but in Hot Springs, Arkansas. They bought a house in the process of being built and made it the base for their next assignment. The assignment carried them not only all over the United States many times, but all over the world again.

Early in the 60s John and Jewell went back to the Philippines to serve as interim pastor of the English-language church in Manila. Throughout the 60s they led tour groups to various mission fields in the Orient and to Bible lands, and in 1967 John was elected second vice president of the Southern Baptist Convention, an honor never before accorded a Southern Baptist foreign missionary.

In 1970, ten years after their retirement, the two of them visited the Korea Baptist Convention and rejoiced to see that old breaches had healed. A bright new fellowship was evident, and they saw signs of a mighty revival.

The night before he left, John said to them, "If I had it all to do over again, I would make the same choices. The missionary task is the greatest calling on earth. It's not always easy; it is sometimes very rough, but God promised to go with us all the way, so we have never hesitated where Christ led. We can only be sure of his leadership; we have not worried but have moved ahead in his name."

In the States at conferences, conventions, and missions emphases John and Jewell have been familiar figures, much in demand as speakers and enjoying a widening group of friends. With growing interest in renewal in the late 60s and early 70s, they were asked often to speak of their experiences in the Shantung revival and of the resources they found in God through his Holy Spirit. They testified of what those days meant to their lives and of their walk afterward. They were one in the spirit.

On March 17, 1973, at the age of seventy-seven John Abernathy was called home to be with the Lord. His last few days in the hospital were hours of victorious witness for his Lord, and his remarks reflected not only a growing awareness of his impending homegoing but also of a growing excitement about it.

Jewell shared those moments with him. Though in declining health, she lives in the home they purchased in Hot Springs. Her enthusiasm still runs high. Her sense of the indwelling presence of the Holy Spirit is obvious with anyone whom the Lord brings her way.

Her eyes literally sparkle as she talks about her ministry of forty years with John Arch Abernathy in China, the Philippines, and Korea.